Gray Wolf

Books by Robert Gray

CHILDREN OF THE ARK

THE GREAT APES

GRAY WOLF

The Natural Life of
North American Wolves

by Robert Gray

W· W· Norton & Company · Inc· New York

First Edition

Library of Congress Catalog Card No. 70-105731

1 2 3 4 5 6 7 8 9 0

Contents

Photographs

Gray Wolf

Part I
The Way It Was

When the white men first came to North America they collided with two of the continent's residents—one a human and the other a wild animal—who would plague them for the next four hundred years. These two residents would fill the wilderness with bloodcurdling whoops and howls; they would harass the white men's herds of livestock; and they would pose threats, real and imaginary, to the settlers' very lives. They were, of course, Indians and wolves.

The presence of Indians in the new land must have been a surprise to the early explorers who had sailed west from Europe expecting to reach India, that exotic, civilized land of silks and spices. They hardly were prepared to be met by half-naked savages. But, sure that they had landed in Asia, they called the natives "Indians," and the name stuck even after the error in geography was discovered.

Wolves, on the other hand, probably came as no surprise at all. The Europeans were all too familiar with these creatures. They had battled them for thousands of years, all the way from Eurasia to the islands of Great Britain.

The new settlers of North America set out to rid themselves of these nuisances. A continent waited to be won, a wilderness to be subdued and civilized. With a thoroughness which marked most of the white men's activities, they declared war. Four hundred years later, at the beginning of the twentieth century, they had won, and the land was theirs by right of conquest. Most of the Indians and all but a handful of the wolves were either destroyed or pushed into unused corners of the continent.

The Indians were descendants of hunters who had come to America more than twenty-five thousand years ago. These early people crossed from Asia on the land bridge which joined the two continents at what is now the site of the Bering Straits. They probably were following the vast herds of wild animals which migrated into the western hemisphere. In the new land the people spread out east and south, and thousands of years later, when the Europeans came, they were scattered in small tribes and nations clear across the continent. Some were fishermen, some farmers, and some—the most primitive—gathered seeds and roots for food. But the vast majority of the people hunted for a living, and wherever these Indians stalked their game, in the forests or on the grasslands, among the mountains or the tundras of the North, they heard the howling of wolves.

Quite likely this was one of the first sounds to greet early man when he crossed into North America. It would have been familiar, for there also were wolves in the old Asian homelands. In fact, there were few places in all of the northern hemisphere which did not know wolves. In North America they were among the most widely distributed of all land mammals. They lived in the dense forests which covered the entire eastern half of the continent. They roamed the grasslands, the western mountains, and the coastlines. Their range extended northward to the limits of the land itself and southward into northern Mexico. The only places they avoided were the deserts and the tropics. Wolves lived on seven million of North America's nine million square miles.

They have existed for at least one million years. However, their ancestry goes back to the Oligocene period, sometime between twenty-one million and fifty-eight million years ago. Among the many mammals which lived then there was one group known as *Miacids,* the forefathers of modern meat-eaters—carnivores.

Wolves attacking a bison on the frozen Missouri River.

AMERICAN MUSEUM OF NATURAL HISTORY/PAINTING
BY WILLIAM CARY

As these prehistoric carnivores evolved, they split into three main groups: the *Pinnipeds* which are aquatic carnivores and include the seal family; the *Felids,* the cat family; and the *Canids,* the dog family, which includes weasels, bears, raccoons, and ordinary dogs. Wolves are simply wild dogs and are closely related to jackals, foxes, coyotes, the dingoes of Australia, African hunting dogs, the dholes of India and, of course, domestic dogs.

Black-backed jackal (Canis mesomalas).

Arctic fox (Alopex lagopus).

Dingo (Canis dingo).

Maned wolf (Chrysocyon brachyurus).

Aardwolf (Proteles cristatus).

The wolf is strictly an animal of the northern hemisphere, although there are several other species scattered around the globe which bear its name. Africa has the aardwolf, a solitary little creature which lives in a burrow and eats termites and other insects; it is a member of the hyena family. The maned wolf of South America is a rangy, foxlike animal. It lives on the pampas and in swamps and is so shy that very little is known about its habits. The Tasmanian pouched wolf is no more a wolf than its neighbor, the so-called koala bear, is a bear. Each is a *marsupial* with a pouch in which its young develop and as such is closely related to kangaroos, wombats, and America's only marsupials, opossums. The pouched wolf is the largest carnivorous marsupial and performs the same function as actual wolves do elsewhere—that is, it preys on other animals. Although once common in Australia and Tas-

Tasmanian pouched wolf (Thylacinus cynocephalus).

AMERICAN MUSEUM OF NATURAL HISTORY/DRAWING
BY CHARLES R. KNIGHT

mania, the pouched wolf is found only on the latter island today and even there is extremely rare. Man and his dogs have all but exterminated this strangest of all so-called "wolves."

The true wolf is called *Canis* by taxonomists, those scientists who classify life forms according to the differences or likenesses between them. So far as we know, there are only two species of wolves: *Canis lupus,* the gray wolf, and *Canis niger,* the red wolf. Canis lupus lived throughout Europe, Asia, and North America before man declared war against him. Canis niger had a much more restricted range—the southeastern part of the United States—and now is confined to eastern Texas and western Louisiana. Many scientists think that the red wolf is merely a cross between the gray wolf and his little cousin, the coyote. This interbreeding, or *hybridization,* can occur among all dogs. For instance, the wolf's closest relatives among domestic breeds—the Huskies, Malemutes, and Samoyeds—are the results of hybridization.

The first true wolves, called "dire wolves," appeared on earth during the Pleistocene epoch, beginning roughly one million years ago. This was the time of the ice ages when great glaciers inched out of the polar regions to cover much of the earth's surface. Four separate times they advanced, buried the land, and then withdrew. The last withdrawal is still going on. Those periods when massive tongues of ice intruded far into the earth's temperate zones must have been years of great hardship for living creatures. The temperature dropped and stayed below freezing for centuries; lakes and rivers froze: ice and snow covered the land. Many species of animals became extinct. One species to disappear was an ancestor of the horse which lived in prehistoric America. After its passing, horses did not reappear on the continent until the Spaniards brought them from Europe almost a million years later.

A prize-winning Siberian husky dog.   MR. AND MRS. LOUIS ANDERSON

Other animals adapted to the severe climate of the ice ages by growing heavy coats. One of these, the musk oxen, exists today in the Arctic. There were many large, hairy mammals during the Pleistocene—mastadons and wooly mammoths, ground sloths twenty feet long, bison with horns which spanned ten feet. And moving among these giants were the predators—stabbing cats (sabre-toothed tigers), weasels, bears, and, of course, the dire wolves.

In time these oversized wolves became extinct and were replaced by Canis lupus. Why did dire wolves disappear? We don't know. Perhaps the harsh climate of the times destroyed the prey animals they needed. In any case, we know of dire wolves only from bones found in tar pits and limestone caves.

Although Canis lupus is smaller than his Pleistocene ancestor, the gray wolf still is the largest member of the dog family.
Even within the species there is a marked difference in size.
The largest wolves are those which live in the far north; they
can grow to weigh one hundred seventy-five pounds, although,
wolves generally weigh about sixty pounds. Their average
length is five feet or slightly longer, and their height ranges
from twenty-six to thirty-eight inches.

Wolves' coloring varies widely from pure black to snow
white and includes all gradations of gray. White wolves are
found almost exclusively in the Arctic, where their color serves
as an excellent camouflage. Most wolves are a mixture of black,
gray, and white with patches of rust or yellow. Usually there
is a tuft of pure black fur at the tip of the tail. The coat is
thick and coarse, especially in winter when the wolf grows an
undercoat to help insulate him from the cold.

A wolf's head is broad with relatively small, rounded ears
which stand erect. He has a long, wide muzzle and a pair of
slanted eyes. His feet are enormous and help support him on
soft ground or snow. He has a beautiful tail, a full brush which
he uses to signal other wolves. Held erect, it usually indicates
that the wolf has dominance within the pack; a submissive
wolf dare not raise its tail when confronting its superior.
Wolves wag their tails with pleasure as domestic dogs do.
Like many mammals, they have a special gland which scents
their urine, and they spray bushes, rocks, and the trunks of
trees as a way of marking their territory, or of leaving a "calling card" for neighboring wolves.

Gray wolves should not be confused with either of their
closest cousins, red wolves and coyotes. Red wolves are much
smaller than gray ones. Coyotes are smaller still and have

Gray wolf (Canis lupus).   GEORGE WILSON

Coyote (Canis latrans).   SAN DIEGO ZOO

markedly different features—large, pointed ears; a slim body; and a long, thin head and muzzle. Gray wolves are almost totally carnivorous, and although both red wolves and coyotes eat meat for the most part, red wolves will take vegetation at times when game is scarce. Perhaps the main reason why gray wolves avoid the deserts is that these hot, dry areas can't support the large animals which the wolves need. So being very wise fellows, they stay away.

Because they are carnivorous, wolves must hunt in order to live. They prefer to take large game since, with a single kill, they get much more meat than by taking a small animal. In the northernmost parts of the Arctic, musk oxen and caribou are their favorite prey, although they will also kill Arctic hares, lemmings, and other small rodents. Farther south the wolves exist on deer, elk, moose, beaver, and even mice. When the white men came to America with their livestock, and especially after they slaughtered the wild game, wolves turned to killing cattle, sheep, and horses.

Herd of musk oxen (Ovibus moschatus). *When threatened, the herd forms a semicircle, a good defense against natural enemies such as wolves but useless when facing men with guns.*

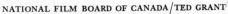

NATIONAL FILM BOARD OF CANADA/TED GRANT

Caribou (Rangifer tarandus).

NATIONAL FILM BOARD OF CANADA

Arctic hares (Lepus arcticus).   NATIONAL FILM BOARD OF CANADA

Opposite: *Bull elk, also called Wapiti* (Cervus canadensis).

MICHIGAN DEPARTMENT OF CONSERVATION

Humans have many myths about the way that wolves hunt. The wolves are said to plan their attacks; to divide their forces deliberately so that some are chasers while others wait in ambush; to hamstring their prey deliberately, that is to cut the main tendons of the rear legs so that the victim is helpless; to seek out pregnant females in order to get at the unborn young; to terrorize their prey by howling; to be bloodthirsty killers.

All of these stories are either distorted or false. In the first place, there is no evidence that wolf packs plan a hunt as a general plans a battle. They are intelligent, but probably not that intelligent. They do cooperate on the hunt; after all, they are much smaller than most of the animals they prey on, and two or more wolves working together have a far better chance of succeeding than one wolf hunting by itself. Even so, they often miss. Dr. L. David Mech, who studied their behavior in Isle Royale National Park, determined that a pack has a hunting success of only 7.6 per cent; that is, it kills its intended prey only six times in seventy-seven tries.

To assume that a wolf deliberately hamstrings his prey is to credit him with far more physical and mental ability than he has. The hunt usually takes place at high speed over uneven ground with the wolf snapping at its prey's belly, flanks, and rear legs. So an animal *is* hamstrung now and then, but certainly not by design.

And while pregnant does are killed, so are nonpregnant females. The animal which is weakest is the one which is felled, pregnant or not.

Opposite: *Moose* (Alces alces).
NATIONAL FILM BOARD OF CANADA/EGON BORK

Are wolves bloodthirsty? They *must* hunt in order to live. But hunting is hard work, and the wolves eat most of what they pull down, although admittedly when game is plentiful they tend to leave more of the carcass than when hunting is harder. In the early days of the West stockmen claimed that wolves destroyed large numbers of sheep just to satisfy a lust for blood. But this argument assigns a human value, lust, to the wolves. Killing is neither good nor bad to them; it is part of their lives. And if there were instances of sheep slaughter, they probably were games to the wolves, not wanton satisfy- ing of bloodthirsty appetites. Of course, this meant little to the rancher who lost his sheep, but we must remember that it was he who invaded the wolves' territory in the first place. He slaughtered the wild game, forcing wolves to turn on his own domestic flocks and herds.

During the countless centuries when man was a hunter, he and the wolves chased the same prey. Wolves fed from the carcasses which men left behind after a hunt, and primitive man probably chased wolves away from *their* kills. About ten thousand years ago a few wolves moved out of the wilderness to join man at his fireside. Maybe these animals were drawn by the bones and other garbage which man tossed aside. Per- haps game was scarce and since man was able to bring down far more than he needed with his arrows and spears, the wolves probably came in to eat the surplus meat. Then, be- cause it was easier to be fed than to hunt, the wolves stayed. With these first stragglers the forefathers of domestic dogs moved in with man. Some scientists claim that the jackal is also an ancestor of certain domestic breeds.

In any case, from that time when the first wild species joined him, man had dogs at his side as he moved across the earth. He has taken them to the Arctic to pull sleds, and he has used them to herd sheep and cattle. The primitive men who originally settled Australia took dogs with them from the old homelands, and from these came today's dingoes, the wild dogs which have destroyed so much of Australia's native wild-life.

Man took his dogs along when he crossed the land bridge from Asia to America, and every Indian village had its pack of half-starved, beaten curs. In Mexico a special breed, the Chihuahua, was developed, primarily for food.

But if Indians abused and even ate their dogs, they assigned a place of honor to wild wolves. That is not to say that they didn't kill them. Wolf skins provided handsome additions to the Indians' clothing, and the brave who wore one was a person of great position. The pelts also helped the Plains Indians get food. These people depended on the great herds of bison which lived then, and many tribes trailed along as the bison migrated with the seasons. They ate bison meat; their clothes and teepees were made of bison leather. Bison bones were sharpened into needles and the sinews used as thread. Bison horns became ceremonial headdresses, and the heavy furs were fashioned into sleeping robes.

But bison were not easy to catch. Until horses arrived with the Spaniards in the sixteenth century, the Indians had to hunt on foot with great difficulty. A large party of braves might be able to round up a small herd and drive it over a cliff, but for the most part hunting was a matter of slow, careful stalk-ing. The wolf, or more specifically his skin, simplified this. Bi-son herds were accustomed to seeing wolves move among them, and the bison sensed whether the animals were hunting or merely walking around. A pack on the hunt caused the bison to run, but individual wolves who were full or merely stroll-ing could move among the herds without causing a stir. The

AMERICAN MUSEUM OF NATURAL HISTORY / PAINTING BY CATLIN

Sioux Indian, concealed in a wolf skin, hunting bison. The artist who recorded the scene included himself in the picture next to the Indian.

Indians knew this, so they took wolf pelts along on a bison hunt. When a brave spotted the herd, he dropped to the ground and threw the wolf skin over his body. Then he crawled toward the bison; when he was within range, he rose and fired his arrows.

Because the Indians lived so close to wolves, observing their behavior and hearing their howling in the surrounding wilderness, the wolf became part of the people's legends and myths. He was admired as a capable and wise hunter. Among the woodland Indians of eastern North America, he was assumed to be the beloved brother of the people's hero, Nanabozho, who was drowned and revived and then became the ruler of the country of the dead. To the Plains Indians, the wolf and coyote were brothers or partners who traveled together sharing adventures. The Tlingit Indians of the Pacific coast had within their culture a Wolf Society which was famous for its healing abilities. British Columbian Indians believed that to kill a wolf would bring a scarcity of game animals to the people. And among some Eskimos wolves were considered to be the gaunt and hungry children of a mother whose family was too large for her to feed properly.

There were one million Indians and twice that number of wolves living peacefully side by side in America in the last half of the fifteenth century. For thousands of years nothing had changed. Season followed season. The grass sprouted, grew, ripened, and died. Trees leafed out, flourished for a summer, aged to the color of old gold in autumn, then stood naked and exposed to the winter storms. Snow fell and spring came again. It had ever been so. There was no reason for either Indians or wolves to assume it would change.

But on the twelfth of October, 1492 a forty-one-year-old explorer, Cristóbal Colón as he chose to be called, stepped ashore onto a small island in the Caribbean Sea. From that moment nothing was the same in North America. A trickle, then a flood of European immigrants followed. They settled the eastern seaboard, poured across the mountains, and spread onto the plains. For four centuries they pressed westward until they owned the entire continent. They built cities and laid railroad tracks. They carved highways through the mountains and raised dams across the rivers. They created nations— Canada, the United States, Mexico, and half a dozen others— that spread from the Arctic Sea to the Isthmus of Panama. By the middle of the twentieth century almost three hundred million people lived on the continent.

All too often greed, ignorance, and cruelty traveled hand-in-hand with the nobler motives of the white immigrants. The dense, hardwood forests of the east were thoughtlessly leveled. The conifers of north and south were felled to the point of extinction. Strip mining ripped ugly gashes in the land. The plains were plowed into wheat fields which blew away when the rains failed. Rivers were polluted, lakes killed, the air poisoned. The Indians were slaughtered, or died in slavery, or became victims of the white man's diseases. The few survivors were herded into concentration camps called "reservations." Entire species of wild animals were destroyed. Of the fifty million bison on the continent when the white men came, fewer than one thousand still lived in 1889. And the wolves, labeled "vermin," were shot, trapped, and poisoned. They numbered more than two million when Colón— Christopher Columbus—landed on that October twelfth. Today a mere handful survive.

Part II
Lupus

Spring

Lupus the wolf pup hung blind and unbreathing deep inside his mother's body. After spending more than two months in the fluid-filled sac which surrounded him, Lupus was ready to be born. Many of the organs vital to his life in the outside world already were functioning—his tiny heart pumped blood; his brain received and sent out messages. Other organs waited—eyes, ears, lungs, and stomach.

The pup had begun life as an egg which was about the size of the period at the end of this sentence. That egg was a treasure house, storing the fruits of one million years of development. For locked into its genes—those precious jewels of evolution—were all the secret prescriptions for bone and muscle, fang and fur, wolf intelligence and wolf behavior. One hundred thousand wolf generations, stretching back to dire wolf and before, had created the priceless recipes, discarding hundreds of mistakes and hoarding the few successes, refining them and passing them on to wolf babies through the genes. The egg which would develop into Lupus inherited this fortune of evolutionary wealth.

Shortly after it was fertilized the egg imbedded itself in a thick, spongy lining called the "placenta" on the wall of the mother's uterus. The placenta supplied the developing pup with food and oxygen from his mother's bloodstream and carried away most of his waste products. An umbilical cord attached him to this source of life. A water-filled sac formed around him, cushioning him from shocks. After he developed into a recognizable, four-legged animal, he grew a coat of soft, wooly hair which would help keep him warm in the world outside his mother's body.

Food, protection, housing. Never again in his life would the pup have these basic needs fulfilled so easily. And that was the purpose of those weeks he spent in his mother's uterus —to give him the chance to develop in safety.

Nature provides most of its creatures with this time before shoving them into the world to fend for themselves. Among insects, birds, and many reptiles the young form inside a hard-shelled egg outside their mothers' bodies, a period called "incubation." For placental mammals, those having a lining on the female's uterus, this time is called "gestation." It varies in length according to the species and usually is longest for larger animals. Elephants, for instance, gestate for twenty-one months, almost two years. Tiny shrews, on the other hand, take only thirteen days for their gestation. The period for humans normally is two hundred eighty days, roughly nine months.

Lupus the wolf gestated for sixty-three days and in that time developed from the tiny egg, barely visible to a naked eye, into a pup weighing more than one pound. As with all placental mammals, his gestation period was the time of fastest, most intense growth.

He was not alone in his dark, warm home. Five other wolf

pups, three females and two males, developed alongside him. For two months these six were nature's most lovingly coddled creatures—unborn animals. But if their gestation was a time of ease for them, it was a period of intense activity for the female wolf inside whose body they were developing.

She was a member of a pack which lived in Superior National Forest in northern Minnesota on the border between the United States and Canada. This forest is one of the few areas in the continental United States where wolves still live. It is a place of low-lying hills, lakes, rivers, and a million acres of trees. Lake Superior lies a few miles to the southeast. Westward, beyond the forest, the continent's Great Plains stretch over the horizon. Directly south, neat dairy and vegetable farms checker the land.

A century ago the forest was a dense stand of virgin conifers—pine, spruce, balsam fir, cedar, and tamarack—and aspen, birch, maple, willow, ash, cottonwood, and other deciduous trees. But during the nineteenth century the loggers came and for more than fifty years ruthlessly slashed at the forest. It took nature almost one hundred years to repair the damage, and even today the scars remain. But under sensible management much of the old growth has returned and with it most of the wildlife species which lived there in the old days.

The wolf pack was one of several packs which roamed the forest. It contained nine animals, about the average number for a pack. There were three adult males, four adult females, and two one-year-old pups. The pack's leader was a large, black male. He was the father of the six little pups which were developing inside their mother's body. She, in turn, was the dominant female of the pack to whom the other females and both yearlings submitted. One of the adult males was a middle-rank individual and the other was a bachelor who had lost his mate several years earlier and whose status in the pack was slipping because of his advanced age. He was the favorite "uncle" of each year's litter of new pups and seemed to delight in caring for them.

The pack's social structure was carefully defined. Big Black was the unquestioned leader. But if his rule was absolute it was also benevolent, for, as all wolves, the members of the pack were great friends. Because they lived their entire lives within the pack each knew his place and stayed there. Big Black had no need to constantly remind the others of his dominant role. The pack shared the responsibilities of the hunt and of caring for pups as they came along. When the wolves rested there was a great deal of friendly shoulder bumping and muzzle nipping, tail wagging and rough-and-tumble play. Only one member was excluded, the smallest of the yearling pups who had been forced into the lowest social position of underdog. Normally she would have spent her entire life there, but Old Uncle was becoming weaker each month and would one day take her place.

When Lupus and his litter mates were conceived in mid-February, snow covered the hills; the streams and lakes lay frozen in their beds; birches stood slender and bare, mere skeletons of trees, with their trunks and branches white against the dark green of the conifers. The forest was a frozen world of black and white with the colors of spring many weeks away. Early in March the wolves wandered to their den area, a sandy hillside deep inside the pack's territory. A small meadow lay at the base of the hill. A stream meandered across it, flanked by willows. A thick stand of pines enclosed the hill and meadow. In the middle of Den Hill five birches, called "paper birches" because of the white, paper-

GEORGE WILSON

Female wolf in a den awaiting the birth of her pups.

thin strips of bark which peeled away from their trunks, grew in a circle. These trees were the offspring of another birch, long since gone, which had grown in the center of the circle. The pregnant wolf prepared her den at the base of one of the five trees.

It was not the first she had dug. She was eight years old, in the prime of life, and she had already borne three other litters. For each she had prepared a new home.

First she dug a tunnel. It was narrow, less than two feet in diameter, and angled down into the hillside. The wolf crouched on her belly and pawed the dirt away with her front feet. When the tunnel was about twelve feet long, she turned it sharply to the left and opened up a larger chamber. This would be the nursery and was barely big enough for the wolf and the pups she would bear. Tiny feeder roots of the birch growing above hung from the ceiling; an underground boulder formed one wall; the floor was left bare.

There were two other dens in the area, used by the pack in previous years. When the female finished the new home, she cleaned out the old tunnels. The work took more than a week of digging, and all the while the rest of the pack lay around in the sun or nosed through the meadow for mice. The usually cooperative pack did not help in the digging of the dens.

Scientists who have studied the behavior of wolves do not know why the pregnant females are left to prepare the dens by themselves or why there are usually several located in one area. Perhaps this is strictly a female's work; because of the subtle chemical changes her pregnancy has worked within her, she probably knows more about it than any other member of the pack. Maybe she prepares several in order to take care of emergencies—flooding, intruders—or simply as extras in case one becomes too soiled from the pups' waste. Often the extra dens are not even used.

Wolves do not always dig their own dens. They might take over and enlarge a fox's burrow. Or they might move in among the roots of a fallen tree or into a natural cave. In the Arctic wolves often burrow into the low hills, called "eskers," left by glaciers which retreated thousands of years ago.

In April, when the birth of the pups was at hand, spring had slipped into the forest. Day by day the snow melted away from all but the most heavily shaded areas. Buds appeared on the branchlets of willows and birches. The ice melted from the streams. And the south slope of Den Hill became a warm loafing area where the pack lay dozing. The pregnant wolf crawled into her chamber to await the birth of her six pups. The moment had come for Lupus to enter the world.

The five other pups who had developed beside him were born first. One, a small male, was stillborn, having suffocated in the birth process. The others came rapidly and were at their mother's nipples by the time Lupus began his short, hazardous trip from the uterus. It should have been uneventful, but the pup was very large and his mother, already exhausted from bearing the five others, was unable to force him out. He hung up in the birth canal. This is what had happened to the first pup and could be extremely dangerous. Each pup had only a few moments grace from the time he was torn free of the life-giving placenta until he *must* take his first breath. He received no more oxygen from the mother's bloodstream, but he could not yet breathe on his own. If he stayed too long in the tight birth canal he would smother. Lupus lay squashed inside the sac of water in which he had developed. Precious seconds passed. Then the moth-

Female wolf and newborn pups in the den.   GEORGE WILSON

er's muscles recovered enough to contract. The sac ruptured
and spilled its fluid into the birth canal, lubricating it. The
muscles contracted again. Lupus was forced ahead. Another
contraction. His head appeared and, with a final squeeze of
the mother's muscles, he was spilled onto the nursery floor.
He gasped and took his first breath.

The world he entered was bare and cold. He lay on sand; a cool breeze passed over him; somewhere in the darkness of the cavern his mother's panting came to his ears. He opened his mouth and whimpered, a tiny, high-pitched whine. Then, with the blind instinct of the newly born, he began to make sucking motions and to clamber along the mountain of fur which kept him from a nipple. A large tongue sloshed across his face as his mother began to wash him. He was rolled back and forth, upended and righted again. Fore and aft, belly and back, the tongue slobbered over him. The pup struggled against the monstrous wet thing and tried to squirm along his mother's belly. The female lay back and left him to his own devices. He inched his way along the mass of fur, searching for a nipple. He found a bare spot and began to nurse. But he had guessed wrong; there was no nipple. He worked his way into the tangle of pups already feeding. He pushed them aside and fastened onto a nipple and began gulping the warm milk. In those first few seconds of his life he had learned two things: First, in order to get milk he must find a nipple; second, if he were to have a nipple, he must shove aside any other pups who might be there already. He would have other lessons to learn—thousands of them—if he were to survive.

Like all wolves, Lupus was born almost completely help-less. His eyes were sealed shut, and his stubby legs could barely drag him along. He had a high-pitched, whiny voice which he used to signal his two basic needs—food and warmth. His body was covered with a growth of soft, dark brown baby hair, except for his tail which was naked and ratlike. He had a short, broad head with a pug nose and two tiny, rounded ears. Seen head-on, he looked like a little pig.

During the first days of his life he did little but eat and

sleep. When he was hungry or cold he awoke, whined, and muscled aside any other pups who might be at a nipple. He nursed and then, warm and with a fully belly, slipped back into that long sleep which followed his birth.

On the third day the mother wolf left the den for the first time since her pups were born. They whined and squirmed after her, objecting to being alone, but the female hadn't eaten in all that time and she was hungry. She bowled the pups over and wriggled to the den's entrance. Outside she dug up the meat which had been cached nearby by the rest of her pack.

During the whelping season when the newborn pups still were helpless, the pack carried part of their kill back to the den area so that the new mother could eat without having to travel. The wolves transported chunks of meat in their stomachs, often for miles, and at the den site dug holes into which they regurgitated the food. They covered the holes with dirt, which they pushed with their noses. Because of some chemistry in their digestive systems, this regurgitated meat was as fresh as when it was swallowed. Of course, only soft portions were transported this way; the wolves carried bones in their mouths. But by swallowing the soft meat they freed themselves of awkward loads hanging from their mouths as they ran through the forest. Under normal circumstances, the cached meat would stay reasonably fresh for several days.

When the mother wolf opened the cache, she interested another of the forest's animals in the meat—a black bear recently awakened from her winter's sleep. The bear was foraging through the forest with her two, roly-poly cubs. She was half-starved, for the fat which she had stored away in her body the previous autumn was used up. She would eat al-

most anything—eggs, roots, insects, and especially meat. But
she did little of her own hunting, preferring to scavenge her
food. She smelled the meat stored at the wolves' den site and
wandered downwind along the aroma. She came to the edge
of the forest. There, sprawled near the meat which she
wanted, were nine wolves. The bear barked a warning to her
cubs. WUFF! and the babies shinnied up the nearest tree.
The wolves snapped awake and swung their heads in the
direction of the sound. They saw the bear and caught her
sweet, musky odor. Hackles raised and low growls rolled
from the wolves' throats. The yearling pups backed nervously through the pack. The mother wolf looked up, saw
the bear, and dashed to the den and her pups. Big Black
barked a warning and walked stiff-legged toward the bear.
The other wolves fell in behind him. At the base of Den Hill
they stopped and waited for the bear's next move.

Had she been smarter or less hungry she would have
turned and retreated into the forest. But the aroma of the
meat was too appetizing. She had eaten cached wolves' meat
before when she had raided unguarded den sites. Once she
had even killed and eaten a litter of pups who had been left
alone. So now she waddled ahead. She splashed into the
stream and when she lumbered out among the willows on the
opposite shore, Big Black charged. His lips were drawn back
and his tail plumed behind him like a war banner. The bear
reared onto her hind legs and held her front paws apart ready
to crush the wolf. But Big Black knew better than to get
within reach of that deadly hug. He leaped aside and lunged
at the bear's flank. She swung her paws and caught empty
air. Big Black was gone, darting at her other flank. The rest
of the pack dashed behind the bear. They nipped at her
heels, then leaped back when she swung to face them. She

caught one of the females with a blow that sent the wolf reeling into the stream. Unhurt, the wolf bounded back into battle. Old Uncle grabbed one of the bear's heels and clung grimly until the bear flipped him away. The pack danced around the clumsy bruin, dashing in to nip her, leaping back when she swung on them. She was far more powerful than the wolves and could have killed any one of them with a single squeeze, but she was no match for their speed. The wolves knew this. Step by step, they forced her back toward the stream. The bear slipped on the bank and tumbled into the water. The wolves pounced on her. She shook loose and backed onto the far shore. A final bite from Big Black spelled the end. The bear dropped to her four feet and waddled toward the forest with the wolves nipping at her heels. She swung around at them a final time then raced into the woods. The pack sat watching until she disappeared and then trotted back to the den and its undefended mother and pups. Deep inside the forest the bear called to her cubs. WUFF! The twins slid from their tree and raced to join their mother. Stinging from a dozen wolf bites, she led them away.

While the fight raged aboveground, the mother wolf lay in the den beside her pups. When she had reached them, all but Lupus were crouched against the nursery's far wall. They had heard the pack's growlings and were terrified. But Lupus, even in his blindness, was headed outside, stumbling along the tunnel. His mother shoved him back into the nursery.

She had prepared the den to be easily defended. Its entrance was so small that any large animal must creep to get in. If the intruder were an enemy the mother wolf could slash at him with her fangs while he inched along helplessly.

Now she lay tense with ears raised, staring at the faint

light which filtered into the nursery. If that light were to be blocked out it would mean that something had entered the tunnel. She was ready. The pups squirmed over her, happy again now that the warm, furry body was back with them. They sought her nipples and tried to nurse. But no milk came down. The mother wolf was keyed up, ready to fight. Nursing had to wait for quieter moments. The sounds of the battle aboveground faded as the bear was driven away. Still the female wolf waited.

Suddenly, the light at the end of the tunnel was blocked out. The mother wolf shoved her pups behind her and backed against the nursery wall. A furry head was poked into the chamber. The wolf bit hard. YIPE! The head was jerked back and a soft whine came from the tunnel. Big Black, after beating off the bear, had crept into the den to check on his family. He whined again. The mother wolf lashed out and drove him away. Nobody, not even the pups' father, was welcome in the nursery for the first two weeks of the babies' lives.

The pack forgot the bear incident as soon as the invader was gone. While the fight lasted it was all that mattered. Once finished it was forgotten. Fifteen minutes later the wolves were sprawled on Den Hill lazing in the sun. The female who had been flung into the water licked herself dry. Big Black nursed the cut lip which the mother wolf had given him. And inside the nursery the female lay back. The fire in her eyes softened as the pups squirmed over her. They fastened onto her nipples and began to suck. This time the milk came.

In the few weeks since the female had dug her den, winter had moved out of the forest. The five birches on Den Hill were leafed out and looked like fifty-foot-tall bouquets of springtime greenery. Delicate, new grass grew at their bases.

Catkins, called "pussy willows," formed on the willows which flanked the stream. And the pines which enclosed the den area stood rank on rank, crisp and military in their forest-green uniforms.

A gaudy, electric-blue Steller's jay flashed across Den Hill, bound on an endless errand of food gathering. In its nest among the pines three hungry chicks waited to be fed, little tyrants who demanded a constant supply of food. Four robins industriously worked the moist slopes of Den Hill for earth-worms. They hopped along, stopped, cocked their heads, and then jabbed into the wet earth. Out came the worms, moist and pale, struggling against the tugging birds. A pair of scar-let tanagers darted back and forth, carrying grass for their nest. They were brilliant scarlet birds with black wings and tails. Newly arrived from their winter home in the tropics, they worked with single-minded concentration to build a nest for the eggs already forming inside the female. Above a quiet backwater of the stream clouds of male, lacy-winged mayflies fluttered in the sunlight, waiting for the females of their species to join them. A great-crested flycatcher, yellow-bellied and rusty-tailed, darted from the forest. It scooped up a mouthful of the mayflies and flashed back to its perch. Along the banks of the stream a gathering of frogs sat wet and bleary-eyed in the sun. In the water around them masses of their eggs floated in transparent jelly, slowly developing into tadpoles.

Over it all hung the sounds of spring—the droning and buzzing of insects, frog croakings, jay squawks, robin trills, the gurgling stream, and the sigh of a warm breeze among the trees. For most of the animals—birds and insects—it was a busy period. There were matings to accomplish, nests to build, eggs to lay, mouths to feed.

But for the wolves it was a lazy time. They lay scattered on

Den Hill, bellies filled from successful nights of hunting, backs warm in the sun. Big Black lay near the den entrance, his large head stretched forward onto his legs. The two other males slept on their sides, rousing only to move when the sun slipped behind a tree. The females sprawled lower on the hillside. One awoke to scratch a flea. Her leg pounded against the side of another wolf who was sleeping beside her. The sleeping female awoke, looked resentfully at the thumper, yawned, and dropped back to sleep.

By the end of his first week Lupus had investigated the entire nursery and was squirming into the tunnel. His hearing, which would become extremely keen as he developed, already caught the sounds of the world outside—birds, insects, and the other wolves moving about. His little pug nose picked up scents which drifted into the nursery—the cached meat, the pine forest, new grass, the moist meadow. And behind his sealed eyelids he sensed light, a dim glow which filtered along the tunnel from the outside world.

Then when he was two weeks old, a most important event took place in his development. His eyes opened. Not in an hour or even a day. But gradually, the dim glow brightened as his sealed eyelids parted. Two pale eyes appeared in the dark brown hair on his face. Milky and unfocused, they saw no details—not the earthen floor of the den nor the rootlets hanging from its ceiling, not even his mother. It would be several weeks before he could see clearly. But the indistinct glow coming along the tunnel touched an instinct deep inside the tiny pup—a drive for freedom and movement. Within a week, Lupus was on his way. He wobbled from the nursery and along the tunnel, stumbling ahead on oversized feet and undersized legs.

At the entrance he was stopped by a mountain of black

hair which blocked the tunnel's mouth. Big Black, the pup's father, was lying across the entrance. Lupus blundered into him, caught his strange odor, and leaped back. His legs gave way and he rolled down the tunnel, half scared, half angry. He struggled to his feet and backed against the tunnel wall, growling and baring his tiny milk teeth.

Big Black peered at his son, first in bewilderment then with obvious delight. This was the first time he had seen the pup. He squirmed into the tunnel, whining in the high-pitched voice with which wolves talk to their young. His rump stuck outside the tunnel, and the frenzied wagging of his tail acted like a signal to the other wolves. They came running, for the birth of a litter was the most important event in the pack's life.

Lupus was overwhelmed. His father's big, black face towered over him; its tongue slobbered across him, reeking of an odor not at all like the pleasant milky smell of his mother. And beyond the face other smells and strange sounds crowded the tunnel's entrance. It was too much for the pup. With a squeal he stumbled back toward the nursery and his mother.

But she was busy with the other pups whose eyes also had opened. She nosed them along the tunnel and Lupus was shoved out with the others. The mother wolf had spent more than three weeks crouched in the nursery. Now she wanted to stretch her legs and turn the pups over to the care of baby-sitters.

At the tunnel's entrance she washed them thoroughly as though they were going to a party, which indeed they were —their coming-out party. Then, with the pups lined up spick-and-span across the mouth of the den, she stepped aside and left them to their admiring father, uncles, aunts, and cousins.

The pack was ecstatic. They crowded against each other, struggling to get at the pups. They whined and licked the tiny bodies, and the one-year-olds became so excited that they chased each other around and around Den Hill. While the mother went to one of the food caches to eat, Big Black sat beside the tunnel in order to keep the pups inside, for they still were too young for the outside world. But he had little trouble with them. The poor pups, abandoned by their mother to such a wild company, huddled against each other. All but Lupus. He struggled onto the mound of dirt piled at the tunnel's entrance and started down its outer slope. His father reached down and grabbed him, and the pup disappeared in the wolf's huge mouth. His head and front legs hung from one side and his rear from the other. He seemed about to be bitten in half. But this merely was the way that wolves carry their babies before the youngsters can move around by themselves. Very gently, Big Black carried Lupus throughout the pack to be admired. He set him down for the other wolves to fawn over. The females licked him clean again and again. Old Uncle nosed him a few times as though saying to himself, "Well, here's my latest baby-sitting assignment." And the yearling pups tried to play with him. They pushed him and scampered along when he rolled down the side of Den Hill. Big Black picked the pup up from the dirt. He carried him back to the tunnel and plopped him among his littermates. The party was over. One of the females shoved the pups down the tunnel and into the nursery where she lay with them until their mother returned from eating.

From that time the pups were the responsibility and property of the entire pack, and all the adults took turns caring for them either in the nursery or at the den's entrance. Regular pack hunting was resumed with the mother joining in whenever the wolves went on a night's run. When she returned, whatever wolf was baby-sitting left the den and the mother entered to nurse the pups, for they still were not weaned.

At four weeks the pups were fat balls of dark brown fur with little, rounded ears and pug noses. Although they were now allowed to wander over Den Hill, they still could not focus their eyes and they stumbled along on their undersized legs, sniffing each blade of grass, growling at the piles of bones lying near the caches, and falling over twigs as they studied the dim, unfocused shapes in a strange, big world.

Wolf pup, four weeks old. GEORGE WILSON

Even at this early age each was developing a personality uniquely his own.

Lupus was the dominant one. He was larger and more aggressive than the others and he used his weight to push them around. He crowded in first at his mother's nipples, or if others were there ahead of him, he shoved them aside. If one of the pups found a twig or leaf which Lupus wanted, he simply stole it from its owner. If the other pups were sleeping against Old Uncle's warm, furry body and Lupus wanted to be there, he plopped onto the top of the heap and squirmed his way down.

The litter's underdog was the runt of the lot—a shy, little female. She was the last at the nipples and the first to be driven from a favorite sleeping spot. When the pups stumbled across Den Hill after a blown leaf, Shy One brought up the rear. When danger threatened she was the first to scoot for home.

The flirt of the litter was a roly-poly little female who was marked for life by Lupus one day. She was playing around Old Uncle when Lupus bumped into her and bit her ear, almost tearing it off. From that day the ear flopped alongside the pup's head like a furry rag waving in the wind. But the accident did nothing to dampen her spirits and Flop Ear became a favorite of the adults, possibly because she seemed to delight in pleasing them.

The second male was a mean little creature whose pastime was to ambush his brother and sisters. When one of them came near, Meanie dashed out, slashed with his needle-sharp baby teeth, and then scooted for the safety of an adult's legs. But he never played with the other pups and lay sulking between his nasty ambushes.

Finally, the last pup was a female who would have been

called a "solid citizen" had she been human. She went about her puppyhood with no frills or special traits, good or bad. She played with the others but without the bounce and joy of Lupus or Flop Ear. When she nursed she sucked with a dogged purpose, and when she was full she fell asleep in the same, plodding manner. If she survived to adulthood she would slip into the pack's middle ranks, neither high nor low. Solid Citizen would go about her business in a matter-of-fact manner and would expect others to do the same.

These endless hours which the pups spent in play were not merely for fun. Nature was teaching them. Eyes, ears, and noses developed rapidly. Muscles grew from the running and jumping. Each grab by a tiny mouth strengthened the jaw muscles on which the pups would eventually depend for food. And just as a kitten—by pouncing on his mother's tail or on a ball of yarn—learns the leap that will some day pin its prey, so the pups leaped at twigs and leaves, readying themselves for the hunt.

But they were still babies, totally dependent on adults as the night of the big storm demonstrated.

The storm had been building all afternoon, massing clouds like piles of dirty wool on the southern horizon. By sunset the clouds had marched halfway up the sky—great, towering thunderheads with their caps torn away by the wind and ablaze in pinks and scarlets in the setting sun. Lightning cracked from their undersides and darted earthward where it shattered trees and smashed against granite outcroppings. The wind sighed among the conifers and whipped the birches back and forth. The forest's animals sought shelter. Frogs plopped into the streams where their newly hatched tadpoles hid among reeds. Birds clung to branchlets or huddled over nests where fledglings peeped in terror. Upstream, a beaver quit felling saplings and swam out to his lodge. And in the wolf's den the female gathered her pups close to her to wait out the storm.

In mid-evening a bolt of lightning struck one of the pines at the edge of Den Hill. An explosive roar and flash of light filled the tunnel. The pups yelped and snuggled against their mother. Lupus shoved Shy One aside and burrowed deeper into the safe, warm fur. Outside, the stricken pine fell across a small ravine which ran along one side of Den Hill.

By midnight the wind had risen to gale force. It flattened the grass in the meadow and lashed at the willows lining the stream. The birch trees growing above the den were doubled to the ground. The wind died for a moment and they snapped upright, only to be forced down by the next blast. When the mother wolf had dug out her den a month earlier, she had loosened some of the roots of one of the trees; now as it was beaten back and forth, its other roots worked free of the earth. The birch began to lean farther with each gust of wind.

The wind brought rain with it, solid sheets of water that hammered against the forest. The earth still was saturated with water melted from the winter's snow and thus could not soak up any of the rain. Rivulets began to trickle among the piles of old leaves. They flowed toward the ravine which bordered one side of Den Hill. Normally the ravine could have handled the run-off but now the lightning-felled pine lay across it. The pine's branches and needles lay mashed beneath the weight of the trunk, and when the first surge of water came, carrying with it twigs and leaves, a dam was formed. The water backed up and spilled across the face of Den Hill. It raced down the slope and among the five birches. At the foot of the loosened birch, some of the water followed the roots down toward the nursery, further loosening the tree. Inch by inch, the birch lost its hold on the earth.

Inside the den each rootlet hanging from the ceiling became a faucet dripping water and mud onto the pups. The nursery floor turned into a sloppy, mud-soaked puddle. The stream outside cascaded over the tunnel's entrance and ran back into the den. The pups climbed onto their mother in a vain attempt to stay dry.

Finally she had enough. She scooped up one of the pups and half-dragged, half-carried it along the tunnel. At the entrance she scooted under the miniature waterfall. Then she raced across Den Hill to one of the two other dens she had cleaned out before the pups were born. After dropping the pup in the warm, dry nursery chamber she ran back to get another. She rescued all but two of them before the weakened birch fell.

When the tree went down, only Lupus and his brother Meanie were still inside the den. Lupus clung to a narrow shelf halfway up the boulder which formed one wall of the nursery. He had shoved his brother from this spot after their mother had left with the other pups. Meanie was left to wallow in the mud and water on the chamber's floor. As the birch tree above them fell, the nursery ceiling collapsed, sending an avalanche of dirt and water down over the unfortunate pup. Lupus, protected by the rock, was trapped in a tiny air pocket.

The frantic mother wolf dashed into the tunnel to get her pups but was stopped by a pile of dirt. She backed out, ran onto the hill above the destroyed nursery, and began digging in the hole left by the fallen birch. She opened the air pocket and dragged out a half-dead Lupus. When the rest of the pack straggled home from their hunt the next morning, she

Wolf pup, six weeks old. ROBERT GRAY

still was digging, searching for the little lost pup.

By midday Lupus was romping with his sisters in the bright sunshine which followed the storm. Like all wild animals, he lived in the present, any moment of which could bring the same fate which had fallen on his brother. The first law of nature was to stay alive. The strong, the swift, and the intelligent might survive; the weak surely would not.

During the next month the pups developed rapidly. Eyesight, hearing, and sense of smell seemed to improve hourly. And the alertness which nature demanded of them if they were to live became a constant companion which sent them tumbling into the den at the first strange sight, sound, or odor. But nature also required that they be very inquisitive if they were to develop into capable hunters, so no sooner had the pups dived into the safety of the den than they popped their heads out to learn what had caused their fright.

When they were eight weeks old the pups were almost completely weaned and were eating meat. The rest of the pack was thin from hunting for them and their mother. During the whelping season they had hunted near the den site, so the game supply was depleted and difficult to find. The time had come for the wolves to move. One day in early June when the pups came out of the nursery for their morning romp, Big Black led the pack down the hill and across the meadow. At the edge of the forest he stopped to let the pups and their mother catch up. The pups were nervous and unsure of what was expected. Only the fact that their mother was nosing them along kept them from running back to the den site with its grass and sunny meadow, the only home they had known. But the nursery was too small for them now, and the game animals which the pack needed had been hunted out. They must move on. The mother called to them in her high-pitched whine and the pups obediently followed her into the forest. The pack would not return to Den Hill until the next whelping season, nine months in the future.

Summer

In June the daylight hours grow long in the earth's northern hemisphere. Along the forty-fifth parallel of latitude, that imaginary line midway between the equator and north pole, the sun rises about four o'clock in the morning and doesn't set again until almost eight in the evening. The earth warms, and in the forest a flurry of activity sets in, for the season will be as short as it is intense. Pines send up tiny branchlets that look like pale green candles. The deciduous trees—birch, poplar, ash, and the others—grow heavy with the year's crop of leaves. Moss clings to rotting logs in the forest's moist, dark corners. Along the watercourses clumps of grass sprout up between the clutter of rocks which the streams have piled, pell-mell, in their beds.

In Superior National Forest one of these streams dashes for several miles down a steep-sided canyon. The canyon opens onto a small meadow where the stream meanders back and forth between hummocks of sedge and grass, slowed by tendrils of watercress growing in its bed. At the meadow's lower end there is a lake with a fleet of water lilies floating on its surface. In summer the lily pads grow large and overlap each other, often closing off the lake from the sky. A log, forgotten by timber cutters of years past, lies rotting on the shore. A few feet away a lone pine tree stands on the slope which clings to the forest's edge. It was to this tree that Big Black led his pack after leaving Den Hill.

He had taken them downstream on a trail which ran along the bottom of the canyon. To the little female pups it was a frightening, dangerous trip and they stayed close beside their mother. But Lupus was in his glory. He sniffed at each tree and bush; investigated the dark, mysterious crevices between rocks; nosed aside pinecones; and pawed into the gravel bars along the stream bed.

He saw a mole snuffling through the litter on the forest floor. He heard a squirrel chattering from the safety of a tree. A covey of bobwhite broke cover and scurried after their mother, and Lupus heard the soft CHUK, CHUK, CHUK of the hen calling her brood. The pup had never seen any animal except the wolves of his pack, yet a deep-seated instinct already was churning inside him; the hunter he would become was developing.

Pine Tree Meadow was three miles below the old densite, and when Big Black finally stopped in the tree's shade, the four pups dropped exhausted to the ground. Months later as fully grown wolves, they would be able to travel forty or fifty miles a day without rest, but now their legs still were weak and undeveloped. They curled up next to their mother, nuzzled her nipples—more for comfort than milk—and fell asleep.

The meadow would be the pack's base of operations for the next few months until the pups were old enough to travel. Normally, the pack constantly wandered through its territory in the forest, seldom spending two nights in the same place. But in spring and summer, while the pups were growing, the pack stayed close to either the den or one of the base camps. They used Pine Tree Meadow year after year as a rendezvous area in which to gather after brief hunting excursions. It was a loafing spot and an outdoor school for the pups' education. It had been chosen carefully. The ground near the pine tree was well drained; the tree's shade gave protection from the hot summer sun; the site offered good visibility. Intruders could be seen and turned away well before they reached the pups, who were in need of special protection now that they no longer had the den to scurry into.

The meadow also had the freedom which the pups needed. While the old den had been safe and large enough for the newborn wolves, it was too confining for two-month-olds. Here on the meadow there was plenty of room, and the pups responded to this freedom. Their chubby bodies of early puppyhood became awkward and gangling; puppy coats were

Zoo-bred wolf pup, ten weeks old.   ROBERT GRAY

replaced by the thick fur of adult wolves; eyes grew clear and bright; the large, oversized feet, typical of mature wolves, developed; tails began to fill out into the beautiful, full brushes carried by adults. And ears grew, and grew, and grew until they dominated the pups' heads.

These developments followed one another in the strict schedule dictated by genes inherited from one hundred thousand generations of wolves. The pups must develop physically and learn the skills needed by the hunters they were to become. Senses must be sharpened; muscles and bones must grow tough and hard; baby teeth must be replaced by permanent incisors, canines, and molars. The pups must learn to coordinate their bodies; make decisions in a wink; and face new, unexpected situations. And they must accomplish all of this in the few weeks of summer and early autumn before winter chilled the forest. Only those who passed the tests which lay ahead could expect to survive.

Lupus bounded into each day as though it were a new adventure designed especially for him. Big ears erect, oversized feet stumbling on twigs and rocks, he dashed into the meadow, back and forth, nosing the grass for the delicious odors it held. A mouse's trail. A dead frog. The rotting log with its household of termites. A pinecone. Day by day the pup worked farther afield. He found the lake and the little stream which emptied into it. One morning, from the shelter of a bush, he watched a family of otters sliding down a mudbank. The happy-go-lucky otters clambered up the bank on their webbed feet, poised at the top, then slid down into the water. With a flick of their tails they bounded back onto the bank and played the game again. Lupus watched for several minutes, then stumbled out of the bush to investigate the strange creatures. One of the otters saw the pup. FLOP! The entire family disappeared into the water. But they were very curious animals and poked their flattened heads out of the stream to see what had disturbed their play. Lupus galloped to the water's edge for a closer look. PLOP, PLOP, PLOP. The otters were gone.

During another outing downstream from Pine Tree Meadow, the pup saw a creature which was far more dangerous than any other he would ever meet. Lupus was nosing among the thick willows that bordered the stream when he first caught the new animal's scent. He crouched out of sight and watched the stream. Around the bend came a strange being. It walked on its hind legs and carried its head erect at the top of its spine. In what would normally be its front paws it carried a long pole with a line attached which it whipped back and forth into the stream. Lupus cocked his head and studied the strange creature. It neither looked nor smelled like any other he had yet encountered. Some instinct deep inside him said to stay low, out of sight. The two-legged stranger worked its way downstream, flicking the line on its fishing pole into the water. When the creature disappeared around the bend, Lupus scooted for home. He had had his first brush with his only enemy—man. It would not be his last, and of all the dangers Lupus would face in his wilderness home, none would be so deadly as that presented by the two-legged killer. His instincts had served him well; the best thing was to keep out of sight.

It was dinner time when he arrived at Pine Tree Meadow. Now that the pups were weaned, meat was their only food. But they were still too young to hunt for themselves, so they depended on the adult wolves. Each grown member of the pack helped feed the babies by carrying meat back to the rendezvous area. When they were within earshot the adults

Wolves are very curious animals. This zoo-bred pup investigates a knot hole.

howled to the pups, who answered and came running. They dashed up to the adult and bit his muzzle and neck, as though pleading, "Feed me." The adult regurgitated the meat he had carried back in his stomach, and the pups pounced on it with much tugging and growling.

A few days after arriving at Pine Tree Meadow, the pups participated for the first time in the pack's community songfest. Back at Den Hill, while they were still confined to the nursery, the pups had heard the singing outside, and by the time they were four weeks old they had tried to chime in. But their voices were thin and high-pitched, not at all like the full, round sounds that poured from adult throats.

The songfest was a ritual which the pack engaged in before hunting. With the pups weaned and more able to care for themselves, the adult wolves returned to their normal routine of searching for game—white-tailed deer, moose, beaver, rabbits, and the other large rodents that lived in the forest. They usually went out as a pack late in the evening and each expedition was the occasion for group singing.

It began when Big Black awoke after an afternoon's nap in the shade of the lone pine. He roused himself and moved among the pack, stopping to lick one of the pups or bump shoulders affectionately with their mother. The rest of the pack yawned, stretched, and scratched at the fleas which bothered them during the summer. They wandered toward Big Black, who had stationed himself in the meadow.

The singing might start with anyone in the pack. Somewhere in the friendly, milling crowd of wolves a head was thrown back, a huge mouth opened, and a howl raised to the sky. It started low and full-bodied, climbed rapidly to a high note which was sustained for half a minute or more, then faded away into silence. Before it was finished another voice joined in, then another and another, each with a slightly different quality or pitch. Some of the wolves sang in deep, full-throated bassos which seemed to support the higher voices. Others were solos, climbing up to swoop and soar above the chorus. Some sang in shimmering tremulos. Some "mouthed" their howls, which gave the sound a hollow resonance. The

A group songfest.   GEORGE WILSON

A wolf "mouthing" its song.   GEORGE WILSON

singing carried for miles into the forest, a wild, free symphony that many people consider the most beautiful sound in nature. The howling was unique to wolves—not like the high, thin yipping of coyotes and certainly not like the howls of domestic dogs. Once heard, it could never be forgotten.

During the singing the pack milled about with closed eyes and wagging tails. Shoulders were bumped affectionately and bodies pressed closely together. The wolves were among the most highly socialized of all wild animals and they thoroughly enjoyed these moments spent together in the songfest.

It lasted for one or two minutes then faded away. One or another of the wolves might start again and the pack would join in or simply ignore the new song, depending on the members' moods. When the singing finally was done for the day, the adults moved out to hunt, and the four pups, sometimes with an adult left behind to watch them, stayed on the meadow.

They enjoyed playing near the stream, where they snapped at leaves and other debris which floated by or studied the creatures living near the water. The frogs especially intrigued them. When one was discovered sitting with half-closed eyes on the bank, it was stalked as though it were a deer or moose. The pup closed on it and if the stalk were successful the frog was nosed. At the first touch of the cold, wet snout the frog would hop away and the pup would leap back, ears cocked and eyes sparkling. Another sniff, another hop. Over and over the game would go on until the frog plunked into the stream.

One day Lupus tired of the sniffing game and began to snap at a frog. Of course he killed it. At that moment the hunter which had been stirring within him came awake, and from then on none of the meadow's small creatures was safe.

The next to fall to his attack was a mouse; then another frog. And with each kill the pup's coordination improved. His eyes saw more clearly and judged distances better; his legs pounced on what the eyes had spotted; his jaws snapped shut on what the legs had trapped. The hunter was learning his craft.

But too much success too soon can be as dangerous for a wolf pup as for anyone else. The episode with the beaver proved this.

The beaver was a young bachelor, recently evicted by his parents from the home lodge. Because he was two years old and sexually mature there was no place for him among his family; he was thrown out into the world to find his own stream or lake, construct a lodge, and attract an unattached female to keep house for him. Late one night in July he waddled across Pine Tree Meadow. He discovered the lake at its lower end. The bachelor moved into an abandoned muskrat burrow and early the next morning he was up and working, felling trees. By way of insurance, he had marked the meadow with drops of castor, the sweet-smelling liquid which he carried in his scent glands. To any other beaver the odor would mean that the area was homesteaded and out-of-bounds.

Later that morning Lupus discovered the castor scent. The pup stopped, sniffed at the hummock of sedge which the beaver had marked, and sat back, puzzled. He was familiar with wolves' scent posts around the meadow, for the pack marked its territory by urinating on trees, bushes, and rocks. But the beaver's scent was a new one to the pup. He sniffed at it again. He looked around but didn't see any possible source of danger. Then he rubbed his face on the marked hummock. As all wolves he delighted in rubbing a strange odor over his body, and before he was finished with the hummock, he had rolled back and forth across it, covering himself with the beaver's odor. Reeking of castor, he followed the trail and half an hour later came upon the rodent. It was a meeting ripe for trouble.

Wolves are intrigued by new odors. This zoo-bred pup rolls in a pile of food pellets.

ROBERT GRAY

The beaver was tense because he was far from water. A pond was not merely home for him; it was a place of safety where he could dive beneath the surface, for fifteen minutes at a time if need be, to escape danger. But the lake in Pine Tree Meadow was small with its shores a hundred yards from the nearest stand of trees. During the night the beaver had dug a canal to the group of poplars which he would fell and float back to the lake.

He was a dark brown rodent, the largest in North America. Like all rodents he had chisel-shaped incisor teeth which would continue to grow during his lifetime. The beaver kept them ground down and razor-sharp by gnawing on wood. When Lupus found him he was braced against one tree while he felled another by using his upper jaw as a lever and gnawing with his lower teeth. He had already felled one poplar which lay, ready to be cut into shorter lengths, beside the canal.

Had Lupus been an experienced hunter, the beaver would have posed no problem. But the wolf was only a pup and his most impressive trophy was a mouse. However, this bit of success had gone to his head and, like many youngsters in a similar situation, he was overconfident. When he saw the beaver he leaped onto the fallen poplar tree. His clumsy, oversized feet caught a branch and the pup fell to the other side, on top of the beaver. Both animals were shocked. Lupus yelped and leaped away. The beaver swung around, saw what had landed on him, and immediately ran for the canal. But the tree lay between him and safety. The beaver had to either climb over or run around the end. He chose to run. Lupus dashed ahead of the waddling beaver. The rodent had no choice but to fight.

He was four feet long and weighed almost forty pounds.

Lupus was half that size. The beaver had claws and the wicked, orange-colored incisors. Lupus had only his baby teeth. The beaver was defending himself against what he assumed was a mortal enemy. Lupus was curious, merely playing as he had with mice.

But the beaver was no mouse. He reared back onto his webbed hind feet, supporting himself with his tail. He bared his teeth and prepared to fight.

The wolf pup circled him, head outstretched, sniffing. The beaver turned to follow him. Lupus lunged forward and the beaver raked him with his clawed front feet. Lupus jumped back. He had never encountered a prey that fought. He sat, head cocked, studying the beaver. He dropped to his belly and scooted forward, hoping to avoid the claws. The beaver raked him again, this time across the face. Lupus yelped and leaped away. The beaver ran toward his canal, but now, stung by the claws, Lupus was angry. He charged and grabbed the beaver's flat, naked tail. The rodent swung around and fastened his incisors in one of the wolf's front legs. Lupus tried to leap back, but with the teeth buried in his leg, he fell and rolled, dragging the beaver over on top of him. The incisors were torn free of his leg and Lupus jumped up and ran. The beaver waddled to his canal and dived to the bottom. He was safe. The wolf pup would not attack again that day; he was dashing across the meadow, headed for home to nurse his wounds.

As July drew to a close the forest became very dry and hot. Electrical storms thundered across the sky, starting many small fires. One afternoon a tree near the meadow was struck by lightning and within minutes a cloud of black smoke billowed up. A spotter plane buzzed the fire and its pilot radioed for help. An hour later two truckloads of fire fighters and their equipment rumbled up the old logging road which lay along one side of the meadow. The men jumped out of the trucks and carried a pump to the lake. They strung hoses around the fire and started the pump's engine.

Lupus and the other pups were upstream hunting mice. At the first sound of the engine and the men, they circled back to the far side of the meadow and sat among the trees, watching the activity. The rest of the pack trotted in from a hunt. Big Black studied the situation—the trucks, the fire, and especially the men. He wheeled around and ran into the forest with the pack at his heels.

Although there was no bounty on wolves in the state that year, men still killed wolves on sight. They used guns, traps, poison, and airplanes. Big Black had been shot at several times and he was wise in the ways of the enemy. He led the pack away from Pine Tree Meadow, running with the fast "rocking horse" gallop typical of wolves. Behind him the fire fighters extinguished the blaze and left. But it would be many months before the pack revisited the meadow.

July slipped into August. A layer of dust coated the forest. The flowers of spring and early summer were gone, and the forest was muted in varying shades of green—dark and somber among the conifers; dirty, pale gray in the deciduous trees. Blackberry vines sent their runners out along the ground where they either lay tangled in the dust or climbed into bushes and trees. The smaller streams slowed to a trickle with their banks drying in the sun. Tadpoles, long since changed into mature frogs, garoomped at night among the grass. The game animals—deer and moose—lay up in bushes during the hot, dry daylight hours and came out to feed at evening. Hunting became more difficult for the wolves. Deer fawns were now large enough to dash away as easily as their elders; the moose calves, still not able to take care of themselves, were protected by evil-tempered mothers. The weak and diseased animals of each species had been killed months earlier by the wolves. So the pack turned to hunting smaller animals—beaver, rabbits, and squirrels.

They no longer brought food to the pups, but called when a kill was made. The pups answered the adults' howls and scampered to the kill sites. So long as any game was available in an area, the kill site became a rendezvous and was used as Pine Tree Meadow had been—as a place to leave the pups when the adults went out hunting. The babies were wandering farther now and often had to run a mile or more when dinner was announced, racing among the trees and splashing across streams. Water was no barrier to them, for they were good swimmers. In fact, if wolves found a dead animal floating in a lake, they would often swim out to it and tread water while they ate.

At the dinner table it was each pup for himself. Lupus, of course, did quite well and muscled his sisters aside until he was full. But the little runt, Shy One, got very little to eat. When she finally was able to move in to a rabbit or beaver carcass, just a few bones and some skin were left, hardly enough for a growing wolf pup. Pound for pound, the pups needed even more food than adults. So Shy One, deprived of the food she needed, gradually weakened. One morning in late August the other pups found her body lying in the forest. They sniffed at it and then, busy with their play, trotted on. Of the original litter of six pups, three were left.

In that fifth month of their lives the pups were as tall and long as grown wolves. With their increased size and power their play became rougher and more strenuous than the timid curiosity of early puppyhood. They made wild charges at each other, then pounced, bit, tugged, and raced away. This roughhousing was especially delightful to Lupus and seemed the outlet he needed for his wild energy. He would lie in wait either among the drying grass or hidden behind a tree for one of his sisters to pass. When she was within range he would leap out, bowl her over, and nip her flanks. Often his baby teeth dug deeper than required for mere play and the female pup would yelp with pain. She might become angry and fight back. But it was short-lived, for either Lupus overcame her or one of the adults—usually Big Black—shouldered the youngsters apart.

Even the older wolves were not safe from Lupus' attacks. But rather than knocking them from their feet, he would be sent flying, head over tail, by a powerful bump from their shoulders. He was no longer the lovingly catered-to baby of springtime and the pack made sure he learned proper manners.

But this teaching did not extend to the art of hunting. The pups would have to learn this themselves by watching the adults and by going on endless expeditions against mice, frogs, rabbits, and other helpless creatures. So far as we know, wolves do not deliberately teach their young to hunt. But since they are carnivorous they eventually learn from instinct and their own experiences.

The pups' first hunt as members of the pack came one day late in September.

It all began rather simply. The pups had joined in the songfest when the pack milled about and howled, and their voices were as full and powerful as those of the adults. But when the singing was finished, rather than staying at the rendezvous site as he had done for weeks, Lupus trotted along with the pack. His two sisters held back and then, seeing their brother leave, ran to join him. Although the pups didn't know it, their days of chasing mice and frogs had ended.

The pack was living in a remote corner of the forest where the only sign of man was an unsurfaced, fire-control access road which snaked across the hilltops. Because there had been no fire in the area that summer, the road was unused and knee-deep grass grew along it, making it look like a narrow strip of grain winding among the pines. The grass was dry and golden now in September and each stalk was headed out. Seed-eating creatures came here to feed—birds who clung to the brittle straw as they filled their craws and dainty woodland jumping mice who gleaned the seeds which the birds shook to the ground. There was a trail down the center of the road, beaten through the grass by deer on their way to water.

At one point the road dipped into a small canyon, crossed on a wooden bridge, and climbed the opposite side. A year-round stream flowed in the canyon, choked into its bed by blackberry vines, young poplars, and alders. Where the stream passed under the bridge, Forest Service personnel had cut back the brush; deer came to this small clearing to drink.

The wolf pack knew this. Early in their stay in the area, they had surprised and killed an old doe at the stream. But the hundred-pound deer had lasted for only four days, then the wolves were hungry again. With Big Black at their head and the three pups sandwiched in the column's center, the pack set out down the access road.

They moved in an easy, loose trot which carried them along at about five miles an hour, a pace which they could maintain for hours if necessary. This trot was the gait they used when traveling and was one of the three natural to them.

When they reached the road they slowed to the walk, their hunting gait. They knew that deer would be lying among the brush, awaiting evening to move down to the stream. The wolves began working. Noses to ground, they coursed back and forth near the road, gradually moving in the direction of the canyon.

Lupus was the first to catch a deer's scent. He was working well away from the other wolves near a growth of brush when he picked it up—the same odor he had smelled at deer carcasses in the days when the pack called him to a kill. The pup slowed his walk until he was barely moving. At the edge of the brush he stopped. He raised his head and peered into the thicket. He saw a faint movement of reddish-brown fur. A twig snapped among the brush as the deer caught the wolf's scent. Suddenly the bush seemed to explode and the deer bounded out.

It was a mature, four-year-old buck with a magnificent rack of antlers which trailed shreds of velvet. This soft, hairy skin covered and nourished the antlers while they developed during the summer. Now, in September, the antlers were hard and pewter-bright, except where the shreds of old velvet flapped like torn flags as the deer leaped from the thicket.

He landed on the roadway and, without slowing, bounded toward the canyon. Lupus raced around the bush to head him off, galloping along silently. Contrary to popular belief, wolves do not howl while hunting; they are much too busy running down and killing their prey.

The rest of Lupus' pack heard the deer breaking from the brush and they came running. At its start, the race appeared hopeful. Lupus caught one of the deer's rear legs between his teeth and knocked the buck to the ground. But this was his first deer; before Lupus could follow up his advantage, the

The wolf's main weapon—his fangs.   GEORGE WILSON

buck struggled to his feet, bumping into the pup and sending him spinning into the bushes. By the time Lupus ran
back to the road, the rest of the pack had dashed by. But it
was no use; the deer was gone.

Although wolves are hunters, they are not as well equipped
for their role as other predators. The great cats, for instance, have claws and fangs, and they can sneak up to pounce
on their victims. Wolves have only their legs and teeth. They
are called "cursorial animals," meaning that they are runners
who chase and track down their prey. Their teeth are very
strong and their legs can carry them for miles at a gallop. But
because they are cursorial their hunting record is not very
impressive, and they have to flush and chase many deer or
other prey before they bring one down.

The pack hunted all that day, then in the evening found a
fawn. The young deer bounded through the forest with Big
Black hard on its heels. The rest of the pack, probably quite
by accident, cut across the circle in which the deer was running. When it bumped into them they snapped at its rear
legs and belly, and within minutes after first flushing the
fawn, the wolves were eating. Lupus was one of the pack
members who brought the deer down. In that brief chase and
kill he realized what every mature wolf instinctively under-
stands—the pack, not an individual animal, is the wolf's
basic hunting unit. Several animals working together can do
what no single wolf can hope to accomplish, and the difference between eating and going hungry is often a matter of
how well the pack cooperates.

After they had gorged, leaving nothing of the deer but its
head and stomach, which they never ate, the wolves moved a
few feet into the forest and curled up to sleep. For the pups
it had been a most important day. The old times of being

pampered were over. No more mere playing at hunting; no more being fed by the adults; no more rendezvous sites where the most strenuous activity was a rough-and-tumble wrestle. The warm, comfortable days of childhood had gone as quietly and naturally as summer itself, which day by day was slipping from the forest.

Autumn

The pack split into two groups on the day following the pups' first hunting experience. Lupus, his sisters, and Old Uncle stayed in the vicinity of the access road and canyon; the rest of the wolves moved eastward. Since the pups were no longer helpless the pack was anxious to resume its normal life. For many weeks at Den Hill and later at the rendezvous sites, they were confined to the immediate areas. But this was not their usual pattern. They were travelers moving about in their territory. There were about three hundred wolves living in several packs in Superior National Forest's three million acres, and each pack had its own territory. The pack which Big Black led had a territory of more than one hundred square miles—about ten miles per wolf—and they constantly traveled it, following watercourses, skirting the lakes, and working the canyons for game.

Some wolf experts of a few years ago claimed that a pack of wolves travels a circular hunting route many miles long, taking perhaps a year to make a complete circuit. But more recent studies indicate that pack travel tends to be somewhat haphazard, back and forth, here and there, with many retracings of the same trail. Because of this erratic wandering, wolves might walk many miles in one day—sometimes as much as forty—with relatively little beeline distance gained. They tend to stay close to water, probably because that is where the prey animals are. But in a place such as Superior National Forest, where there are hundreds of lakes and streams, their movement is not restricted to any great extent.

When Lupus, his sisters, and Old Uncle set off on their own, they saw many indications of the richness which autumn brings to the forest. Deer, fat from their summer's grazing, looked up as the little pack walked by and then returned to their eating, instinctively recognizing that the wolves were not hunting. Many prey animals have this built-in warning system. On the plains of Africa, for instance, zebras and wildebeests will graze unconcernedly near a pride of lions whose bellies are full. But as soon as the cats begin to hunt the grazing animals grow nervous and watchful.

As the four wolves walked through the tall grass in the road, tiny woodland jumping mice bounded away on their overgrown rear legs, taking twelve-foot leaps in their panic. A porcupine who was stripping bark from a pine tree barely looked up as the wolves passed. Only an extremely hungry or stupid wolf would face that barricade of quills. Farther down the road Lupus found a fox's carcass. The heavy odor which hung in the area indicated that a skunk had been here, probably feeding from the carcass when an intruder—maybe a raven—had disputed the meal with him. A flattened bit of grass marked the target area of a red-tailed hawk who had spotted a squirrel from hundreds of feet aloft and had plunged onto its victim. Where the road dipped into the canyon the wolves caught a sweet, musky odor coming from the bushes. One of the female pups whined nervously. At the sound a mass of black fur reared up from behind the bush. It had a broad head, little piglike eyes, a wet snout, and a mouth that dripped blue saliva. The wolves had disturbed a black bear as it ate blueberries.

There was no love lost between these two species. Often the bears raided caches of meat stored near the wolves' dens in springtime. The wolves, on the other hand, were great fanciers of bear meat, but except to defend their dens and pups they seldom attacked the extremely powerful animals and depended on carcasses they found for bear meat.

The nearsighted bears were unpredictable at any time of year; they might or might not charge. So when the berry eater rose from behind its bush, Old Uncle stepped between it and the pups for whom he was responsible. The pups whined and backed away. The bear, however, had no intention of attacking; it was interested only in eating as much as possible for the long winter which lay ahead. WUFF! It dropped to the ground and waddled away. The wolves walked on down the road, bound for the little stream at the bottom of the canyon.

Deer, mice, a porcupine, fox, skunk, hawk, and bear—all seen or indicated in one, short stroll. Had the wolves been hungry, they could have made several kills. Truly, autumn was a good time.

Around them the forest was daubed with color—yellows, reds, golds, rusts, and browns. Only the conifers still wore green, their year-round color. But the wolves did not catch any of autumn's colors, for like most mammals excepting the primates they were color blind and saw the world in gradations of black and white.

Yet wolves have extremely keen vision, among the best of all animals. The slightest out-of-the-ordinary movement in the brush, the passing shadow of a bird, or a suspicious rippling of the water arouses their curiosity. And their hearing is unsurpassed. As one wolf expert has expressed it, "Wolves can hear a cloud passing overhead." There is some question about their sense of smell, but certainly it is very good. Any new odor is cause for further investigation, and if it is enticing enough the wolf will roll over and over in it as though to soak it into his fur. By the time the pups are six months old—the age of Lupus and his sisters during that late September—all their senses are well developed.

In fact, as the male pup walked along the access road, there was little to distinguish him from a fully grown wolf. He had long ago lost the fine hair of babyhood and was covered by a magnificent coat of black and white fur. A thick undercoat which would continue to grow and insulate him from winter's cold made him appear huskier than he actually was. This coat would be shed in the spring. He had a broad head with widespread, almond-shaped eyes. A fringe of black hair outlined the eyes and swooped outward onto his cheeks, further accenting the eyes' shape. A patch of black hair grew across Lupus' nose between his eyes, giving him a perplexed or even arrogant expression. His muzzle was wider than that of most domestic dogs or of coyotes, which have long, thin snouts. Lupus' baby teeth still had not been replaced by the permanent teeth on which he would rely for the rest of his life. That would be one of the last stages in his transition to adulthood—aside from reaching sexual maturity—and would take place late in autumn or early in winter.

A ruff of dark gray hair grew around his neck and blended into a gray stripe which extended along his back to the base of his tail. The tail itself was a fine, large, grizzled brush with a tuft of pure black hair at its tip.

Lupus' body was long, almost six feet from snout to tip of tail, and well muscled. As he grew older, he would fill out until as an adult, he would weigh well over one hundred pounds.

The most obvious feature which still lingered of his passing adolescence was his legs. They were thin, lacking the heavy layers of muscle which he would develop during the next few months. It was the relative weakness of these legs which had sent the pup and his sisters to live apart from the rest of the pack. The adults simply could not wait for undeveloped pups to keep up on the trail.

Lupus had very large feet; his footprints spanned more than four inches in diameter. When he walked or ran his feet spread out, giving him additional support, especially on wet ground or in snow. But as the approaching winter was to prove, even these "snowshoes" would not carry him on top of soft, deep snow.

Those weeks which the pups spent with Old Uncle were ideal for the youngsters to perfect the one craft they must learn—hunting. It was as though nature had conspired to provide the best conditions for their education. The temperature was neither too hot nor too cold. Day by day the sun hung lower in the sky—a "dying sun," people called it—and the forest radiated back into space the heat it had accumulated during the short, intense summer. The days were pleasantly cool with the aroma of overripe berries and that indefinable, tangy odor of autumn which settled over the forest. At night dew froze on the meadow grasses; ice glazed the quiet backwaters, imprisoning leaves and twigs; spider webs were transformed, as though by magic, into delicate, frosted lacework. The croakings of frogs and the rasping songs of the insects were gone for the year. The forest lay rich and busy, preparing for winter.

Among most of the animals there was frantic preparation. They became hoarders. Deer and moose spent the daylight hours feeding, building up layers of fat on their bodies. Beavers wandered far from water to fell saplings which they stuck upright in the bottoms of their ponds. Mice stocked underground granaries with seeds and grass. Squirrels poked nuts into their nests and the crevices of trees. The bears stuffed themselves with whatever food they could find—berries, fish, rotting carcasses—in anticipation of their long, winter's sleep. Insects laid the last clutches of eggs for the season and then died, leaving the delicate eggs to endure winter as best they could. Frogs burrowed deep into the mud. Migrant birds formed into flocks for the forthcoming flights south. Everywhere it was hurry, hurry. Winter was coming.

Only the wolves and other predators stood aside from this frenzied activity. Except to grow coats for insulation or camouflage during the winter, these animals had little reason to prepare for cold weather. Their food supply was all around and, in a sense, they lived off the labor of others. Their nourishment depended on a long series of predator and prey relationships called a "food chain," which began with the sun itself.

Any given food chain is quite complicated but, in simple terms, it operates like this for most of land mammals: The sun supplies energy which most plants use to convert minerals and organic material of the earth into food. Grazing and browsing animals eat the plants. They, in turn, are eaten by predators—wolves and men, for instance. When the predators die, their bodies decompose and give back to the earth much of the substance needed to continue the cycle.

So, while the prey animals worked to harvest the plants which would see them through winter, the wolves waited to take advantage of their labors.

Unfair? Not really, for predators fill an important niche in the delicate balance which exists among living things. In fact, and although it might not seem to be the case, they are essential to the prey animals' well-being. The following story is an instance of this and of what happens when an intruder—man, as usually is the case—disturbs the normal relationships of wildlife.

On the northern rim of the Grand Canyon there is a large, tree-covered plateau called the "Kaibab." For tens of thousands of years a herd of exceptionally beautiful mule deer lived there along with predators—mountain lions, bobcats, coyotes, and wolves. Both the deer and the predators prospered, for the numbers of each were balanced by the available food supply. The deer had excellent grazing and were kept in check by the predators. The predators in turn, killed only enough deer to live.

Then, in the latter part of the nineteenth century, white ranchers drove cattle onto the Kaibab. The plateau became overgrazed and the number of deer declined. Concerned for the welfare of the deer and assuming that the predators were causing them to disappear, President Theodore Roosevelt set aside the Grand Canyon—including the Kaibab—as a game reserve in 1906. The predators were destroyed. In the next twenty-five years 5,000 coyotes, 781 mountain lions, 554 bobcats, and 20 wolves were killed. However, the domestic livestock were allowed to remain and, in fact, their numbers increased. So did the deer's. From a herd of three thousand in the early days, the deer population exploded to almost one hundred thousand animals.

The inevitable happened: The deer starved as they and domestic livestock overgrazed the range. Diseased and undernourished animals ate pine needles, dead weeds, twigs—anything. The beautiful Kaibab *and* its deer were being destroyed. State and federal government agencies tried to remedy the situation and finally brought it under control by intensive deer hunting and granting complete protection to the few predators which had survived the earlier massacres. Today the Kaibab has returned to its original condition with predators playing an important role in the delicate balance which exists between living things.

Lupus the wolf pup was a small part of that balance as he moved through Superior National Forest, alert to the snapping of a twig or the rustle of grass which might give away a prey animal. But of course the pup knew nothing of this. He only knew that when he was hungry he must eat and that in order to eat he must hunt. During the weeks that he spent with Old Uncle and his sisters, he perfected his craft.

The four wolves moved into the little canyon which lay across the access road. Many small animals came to drink at the stream, and in those days of late September they were sleek and fat.

The first of these little animals which Lupus killed was a beaver. In contrast to his humiliating defeat of several weeks earlier, the pup dispatched this beaver easily. He found the big rodent in a grove of willows, industriously felling saplings. The beaver was a quarter of a mile from his pond, much farther than he would normally wander, but with winter coming on he had moved out to find food for the long, frozen months. Lupus heard the rasping sound of the

GEORGE WILSON

Wolves hunt primarily at night, moving through their territory at a loose, easy trot.

beaver's incisors whittling away at the trees and, curious animal that he was, he *had* to learn what was causing the sound. He scampered in front of Old Uncle and, for the first time in his life, led a pack on the hunt. From that moment he was accepted as leader of the small pack. The encounter with the beaver was over in a flash. The rodent barely had time to rise on his hind legs before Lupus dashed in on him. With one snap of Lupus' jaws it was all over.

That night, the pack called to the main group of wolves which had worked its way to the eastern edge of their territory, almost three miles away. When Lupus' howls reached them Big Black answered and soon the two groups were calling back and forth. Their howling roused a flock of mallard ducks who were gabbling softly to themselves on a lake. And it disturbed a great blue heron, asleep on one leg in the lake's center. It lasted for several minutes, echoing back and forth in the canyons, and then died away as the two packs, their bellies filled, lay among the forest's litter to sleep away their meals. So long as the pack was split up the two groups would call to each other regularly. The *entire* pack was one family and when some of its members were away the others kept in touch.

A few days after the beaver hunt Lupus saw his first moose. The cow, a one-thousand-pound creature, was standing alongside her adolescent calf in a stream, cropping watercress where the stream emptied into a lake. When Lupus spotted the pair he broke into his rocking horse gallop and seemed to float across the meadow toward them. The cow looked up and immediately placed herself between the calf and the approaching wolves. The baby was still dependent on its mother who, in turn, would face an entire pack of wolves to defend it. But the sight of the wolves caused the calf to panic and it trotted awkwardly toward the lake. Its mother was obliged to run along with it although she knew from experience that the best way to deal with wolves was to stand and face them. Lupus and his pack closed rapidly. The pup leaped at the cow moose, missed, and ended up with a mouthful of hair. Old Uncle, wise from many years of hunting, ran ahead to attack the calf. But the cow stayed close to the baby's rear and when the wolf was close enough to leap, the cow butted him, knocking him off stride. Then the two moose were splashing into the lake and the wolves fell back. The cow and calf swam to the center. The wolves paced back and forth along the shore. They could swim, but seldom pursued their prey into deep water. Their style of hunting was designed for dry land—the chase, the leap, and the bite.

The moose swam toward the lake's opposite shore and the wolves followed around to intercept them. When the cow moose saw this she reversed her course and led her baby back toward the center. After fifteen minutes of this long distance game of tag, the wolves trotted away. They knew better than to spend their energy on a fruitless hunt, for there were other prey animals in the forest. Later that day they found a dead bear and fed off it for almost a week.

One day in mid-October a chilling wind blew from the north. It stripped the trees of their last leaves and carried the debris to the lee side of rocks and hillocks. There, it dropped the leaves onto the rotting litter of former years and in this way added to the natural compost which, season after season, slowly built up the forest's reserve of soil. The wind rustled among grass and sedge, already brown and lifeless on the meadows. It brushed the lakes, raising waves which bobbed hundreds of mallards feeding among the rushes. The ducks sensed the warning carried on the wind—winter was coming. Like one bird, they exploded from the lakes and flew southward. The great blue heron unfolded its six-foot wings and lumbered away. After it was airborne the huge bird drew its head back over its shoulders in the manner of all herons and trailed after the ducks. That night a flight of geese passed over the forest. Their honking woke Lupus. The pup looked up and caught a glimpse of the birds—a broad, V-shaped formation that flittered across the face of the moon and then was gone.

Later that same night the wind brought a light snowfall, the first of the season. But of the forest's thousands of creatures, very few were awake to see it—some small rodents scurrying among the dried grasses and a gray owl who soared over the meadow, hunting them. The snow flurry lasted a few minutes, then passed on. But in its brief passage it created a world unlike any the wolf pups had ever seen. They awoke the following morning to find that what had been brown and drab the night before was dusted with snow—the grass, pine trees, and the hummocks of sedge. The pups cocked their heads and sniffed at the strange white stuff. Lupus tasted it. Satisfied that this new world posed no threat, he began to play. He rolled in small piles of snow which had drifted against rocks and trees. He squirmed into it and lay waiting for one of his sisters to pass. When she came within range he dashed out and threw her with his shoulder. The little female ran and Lupus took after her. The other pup and even Old Uncle joined in and the rough-and-tumble play ranged back and forth through the forest.

But by ten o'clock the sun had melted the snow. The wolves gave up their games and set out to hunt.

That afternoon, after the pack made a kill, Lupus' dominance in the small pack was established once and for all. The wolves hadn't eaten for several days and were famished. But the small beaver they had killed wasn't large enough for all of them. Old Uncle tore away a large piece of meat and carried it away to eat. Lupus turned on him, teeth bared, hackles raised, and tail stiffly erect. A short, noisy fight ensued. In the end, Old Uncle flopped onto his back, belly up and tail tucked between his rear legs. Lupus sniffed him, took away the piece of meat, and ate it himself. Only then did the other wolves crowd in on the carcass. The episode was typical of packs, for often there are brief, bloodless battles over food. The dominant animals always win.

After the brief tussle, life went on as usual within the small pack. No grudges were held and for the few days that Lupus spent alone with his sisters and Old Uncle he did not assert his authority again. There was no need to; it had been established.

Six weeks after the main pack had left the pups with Old Uncle, the two groups came together again. The small pack was standing on a frozen meadow when they heard Big Black calling. Lupus and his sisters answered and their howls rang through the forest as Big Black led his wolves toward them. When they bounded from the forest Old Uncle ran up to the leader wolf, tail wagging and tiny whines of joy pouring from his throat. The two wolves raced across the meadow bumping shoulders and crossing tails, two old friends who were delighted to see each other again. The pups didn't understand any of this. They had lived apart for six weeks and the memory of the pack had dimmed. Now they were surrounded by adult wolves. The two little females crowded together on a hummock, tails between legs while the other wolves sniffed and licked them.

Wolves cross tails affectionately, much as humans hold hands.

Lupus, perhaps a bit intoxicated with his leadership of the
small group, kept his tail raised when Big Black approached.
But something about the true leader's way of moving—his
self-assurance, the raised tail, his quiet dignity—communi-
cated itself to the pup and he lowered his tail and crouched
submissively. Big Black acknowledged this signal of submis-
sion by sniffing his son and then walked past. In time, if
Lupus survived he probably would become the pack's dominant male; he had all the attributes of leadership. But that
time was many years away, and regardless of his role in the
small group, he was still submissive before Big Black.

From that day the two groups were together more often. If the adults wanted to travel particularly fast and far the pups stayed behind, but on the shorter forays the wolves stayed as one pack.

One morning in late November they were trailing along a stream. They stumbled onto a deer hunter cleaning his kill. When Big Black saw the man he turned tail and darted for the woods with the rest of the pack on his heels. At the end of the line was Old Uncle.

After his short stay with the pups, the fifteen-year-old wolf had weakened and was no longer able to keep up with the pack. Arthritis crippled his joints. His teeth were worn back and he could no longer kill. Gradually he became a straggler, the pack's underdog, replacing the little female who had lived in that unenviable position for so many months. For the past few weeks Old Uncle hadn't even been accepted as a member of the pack, and the others tolerated him only if he stayed well back on marches and slept aside during rest periods. He was reduced to eating whatever meat the pack left after a kill.

He could have drifted away and become a lone wolf, but the pack was the only life he knew. Wolves seldom leave their pack to travel alone, for they are among the most social of all wild animals. There are very few "lone wolves" despite man's legends about them.

So on that day when the pack met the deer hunter, Old Uncle trailed behind and it was he who was in sight when the surprised man grabbed his rifle and began shooting. Old Uncle was killed.

With the loss of its underdog the pack's social order was upset and another wolf had to take Old Uncle's place. It was Flop Ear, the mischievous, flirting little female. After the death of Shy One earlier in the year, Flop Ear was left as the smallest and weakest of the season's litter. Because of her size all the other wolves dominated her and gradually she was pushed toward the bottom of the social heap. With the death of Old Uncle she became the underdog, the lowest member of the pack. For the rest of her life she would stay there. She would never mate, for all other females in the pack were superior to her and would keep her away from the males. She would not be allowed to eat with the others or otherwise mingle with them. On the rare occasions when a fight broke out in the pack, she would take the brunt of the punishment as each wolf turned on those below him. She alone would have no one to turn on. Yet, in her own humble way she would be as important to the well-being of the pack as the leader.

A wolf pack is a tightly organized community. It has a leader who is dominant over everyone else. Below him there are many, complicated relationships in which certain wolves are dominant over some and submissive to others. Finally, at the bottom of the social heap is the underdog who is dominant over none and submissive to all. When that animal dies or drifts away another wolf *must* take it place in order for the pack to be a complete social unit.

With the death of Old Uncle, Big Black's pack was reduced to eleven animals. Its average population, year in and out, had always been less than ten. So as autumn cooled into winter the pack spent more time on the trail, running down game to feed the extra mouths. By November the forest was covered with snow that would last until the following spring, making travel more difficult. With the smaller hibernating animals gone for the seasons the wolves turned to their favorite prey—deer and moose.

Those days of late autumn were a final test of all that Lupus had learned. From the moment, months before, when he had killed the frog in Pine Tree Meadow his instincts had driven him with unrelenting persistence in one direction—to become a hunter. The early curiosity that had made him investigate each leaf and blade of grass; the games of tag with the other pups; the nipping and tugging at mature wolves; the babyish stalking of mice and frogs; the first kill; the dismal failure in his first encounter with a beaver; the rough-and-tumble days of autumn—all had been for one purpose. The hunt. He had practiced over and over again; failed many times to succeed once; learned to stalk and lie in ambush, to charge and leap. He had developed powerful jaws and legs; become wise in the behavior of the game animals; perfected his craft. It was all that would stand between him and starvation for the rest of his life.

The first heavy snow fell onto the forest. The lakes and streams froze over. A few sprigs of dead grass poked through the snow which covered the meadows. In his lodge in the middle of a lake a beaver sat on the ledge he had built above the water. He ate a twig of willow which he held between his front feet. There were many more willows waiting to be eaten, stuck into the lake's mud outside the lodge. Along the frozen stream which fed the beaver's pond a snowshoe rabbit, white in his winter coat, hopped along his runway. He bumped into a clump of dry grass, sending a shower of seeds to the ground. A flock of little birds—slate-colored juncos moving south ahead of winter—fluttered to the ground and began pecking at the seeds. Their chirping attracted an ermine. He was one foot long and white as the new snow except for the tuft of pure black hair at the tip of his tail. He crept toward the birds and when within range, tensed to charge. But one of the juncos saw him; it twittered a warning and the entire flock scattered. The ermine moved on. Farther downstream he heard a twig snap behind him and scurried into the safety of the nearby forest. He climbed onto a log and raised his head to see what had caused the noise. A pack of wolves led by a big, black male came into view. They walked along the stream bed, stopping frequently to sniff at old game trails, mark scent posts, and study the forest for game. At the end of the line, well behind the others, a little female wolf with a flopping ear walked alone. Her head was hanging and her tail drooped despondently. The ermine watched from his log until she disappeared, then he slithered to the ground and ran back among the grass to search for rodents in the snow.

Winter had come to the forest.

Winter

Lupus the wolf pup was awakened by the sound of snow
sloughing from a pine branch somewhere in the dark forest
around him. SHOOSH, PLOP! This was his first winter and
each strange, new noise snapped him alert—ice groaning on
the lake, a tree branch breaking beneath its load of snow, the
howling of a blizzard. He studied the fresh pile of snow lying
under a nearby pine. It didn't seem dangerous. He cocked
his head and listened for other sounds. There were none. He
tested the cold air with his nose. No strange scents. Finally,
satisfied that all was well, he stuck his nose beneath his tail
and slipped back into a light, relaxed sleep which wolf experts call the "wolf nap."

A storm had swept through the forest early in the previous
evening, adding over a foot of snow to the more than six feet
which already covered the ground. The storm caught the
wolves resting in the shelter of a cutbank. They were cold-
weather animals with thick, heavy coats, so when the snow
came each wolf merely curled into a tight, furry ball, nose
under tail, and slept comfortably under the insulating white
blanket.

The winter struck very hard. For a month after the middle
of December, great masses of frigid air slid southward from
the polar regions and engulfed the forest. The temperature

skidded far below zero as storm followed storm with monotonous regularity, bringing thick, blinding snow. If the storm moved slowly, the snow fell as large, soft flakes that formed into feathery piles in which the wolves rolled and snuffled. But often the wind rose and the snowfall became a blizzard, tearing at pine branches; whipping the bare willows and birches; and packing white, hard mounds of snow in the lees of rocks and cutbanks. Then the wolves sought the shelter of either the forest or overhanging rocks to wait out the storm's fury. Other creatures of the forest did not fare so well. Insect eggs, lying dormant in their cases on tree branches or in the litter of the forest's floor, froze in the abnormally cold weather. Many of the hardy little forest birds who love cold weather froze or suffocated in the frigid, blinding snowfalls. But of all the large animals, the deer suffered most. They sought sheltered areas where they bunched up to escape the wind. As the snow closed in they tramped out clearings, called "yards," where they could reach up to browse on overhanging trees. But the blizzards piled snow deeply around the yards and the deer were trapped. They slowly starved.

We humans, safe in our heated houses, see winter as a time of sparkling beauty and outdoor sports. But to the creatures who must live outside in a world of snow and bitter cold, winter is the most hostile time of year. Many animals do not live until spring.

Even the carnivores, better off than most, do not find winter easy. Hunting is more difficult. The snow is deep and game hard to find and even harder to catch. Accidents, always a danger to predators, take a heavy toll of lives.

One day in January the wolf pack was chasing a deer. The buck, with its long legs, was covering fifteen feet with each leap; the wolves could bound only about twelve feet. Hard as the chase was for the deer, it was infinitely harder for the wolves. But they had to overtake the buck or miss a meal that day.

The deer left the deep snow of the forest and dashed out onto a lake which had been swept clean by wind, leaving its frozen surface bright and extremely slippery. The deer lost his footing. He fell; struggled upright; and, half-running, half-skidding, fled across the lake. The wolves raced after him, slipping and sliding on the ice. Solid Citizen, the conservative, dignified little female, ran after the deer, galloping over the ice in her dogged, no-nonsense manner. Part way across the lake her feet skidded from under her. As she fell one of her legs twisted beneath her and the weight of her body snapped its bone. From that time Solid Citizen limped along behind the rest of the pack, favoring the injured leg. The deep snow made traveling almost impossible for her and she could no longer hunt or keep up with the pack. As the days passed, her tail drooped lower between her legs and her head slumped forward. She grew thin and weak from lack of food. One morning she was missing. The following spring a fisherman found her wasted body lying beside a stream.

But hard as the winter was there were days when the forest sparkled, clean and fresh in its pure-white covering. That morning when Lupus was awakened by snow sliding from the pine bough developed into one of these.

The storm moved out of the forest a few hours before dawn, leaving the night crisp and clear in its wake. Stars hung like hard, blue diamonds in the bitterly cold air. In the northern sky the Aurora Borealis, the "northern lights," shifted silently back and forth like clothes hanging on a wash line, changing patterns of blues, greens, violets, and white. The forest lay locked in dense blackness, cut off from

ROBERT GRAY

Because of their heavy coats wolves can withstand extremely cold weather.

the sky by the pines. On open meadows starlight glistened from the snow like a million tiny diamonds scattered across the surface. An owl glided across a small meadow, resuming his hunt which had been interrupted by the storm. He saw a hint of movement in the darkness. A rodent was scampering across the meadow, and the owl had spotted the animal's shadow cast onto the snow by starlight. The bird swooped down on wings which were silent as ghosts. He snatched up the rodent and carried it home to a warm nest deep inside a hollow tree. Back on the meadow one of the owl's wing feathers, torn loose when the bird caught the rodent, hung in a sprig of dried grass. A delicate imprint of the owl's wings was impressed in the nearby snow. One by one the stars set in the west; along the eastern horizon a faint light appeared. It grew, climbed the sky, and dissolved the dense blackness of the forest's interior. In that flat, colorless light of dawn the wolves awoke, stretched, and shook the snow from their heavy coats.

The pack was in excellent condition. The snow made hunting very difficult so the wolves visited the deer yards to feed on the half-starved and dead animals there, and while this supply of food lasted they ate regularly. As a result they had thick, healthy coats; bright eyes; and full, rounded bellies. They were ready to start hunting again when the deer yards finally were empty.

That day after the heavy storm would be spent on the trail searching for game. But in the crisp, crystal morning there was time for play. Lupus started it. He was snuffling through the snow, nose buried, rump raised as he plowed along, curious about what might have been buried under the night's fall. He spotted another wolf sitting on the snow, idly scratching an ear. Lupus dropped to his belly and slithered closer.

He tensed and with a furious growl launched himself. All one hundred pounds of his body crashed into the other wolf, bowling it over in the snow. The outraged victim righted himself and lunged at Lupus, fangs bared and hackles raised. The pup raced away. He ran behind a tree and bumped into Big Black. Father and son grabbed mouthfuls of fur and rolled down the hill, scattering the rest of the pack. The original victim of Lupus' practical joke joined the biting, leaping, running scramble. Then, as suddenly as it had begun, the fracas ended. The wolves sniffed each other, nipped muzzles, wagged tails, and trotted up the hill to the rest of the pack. Lupus' mother ran to greet Big Black. She whined with joy and gently bumped his shoulder. He nipped her. Lupus sniffed at a scent post recently marked by one of the wolves. He added his own sign, then fell in behind as the pack filed down the watercourse and into the day's business.

Big Black took them along a trail which the pack had developed. Until the previous night's storm the path was pounded well into the snow, hard and firm enough for a man to walk along, for the wolves used it frequently. They had no liking for the deep, soft snow of the forest and stayed along the frozen watercourses as much as possible where the snow was not apt to be so deep and the ice provided a smooth surface for traveling. The forest's streams flowed into the many lakes in the area and these, in turn, were joined together by creeks or rivers. So while the streams and lakes were frozen over, the wolves had a convenient series of "roads" throughout their territory. But convenience was only one reason for using the frozen waterways; there was another of equal or even greater importance. During winter when deep snow filled the forest, deer and moose moved out onto the open streams and lakes to feed; since the wolves needed

Winter brings deep snow to wolf country.   GEORGE WILSON

these animals for food, they traveled where the deer and moose would be. The pack had no desire to spend its energy floundering among snowdrifts if it didn't have to.

But even along the paths they had pounded out travel was difficult that morning after the storm. More than a foot of snow had fallen during the night and the wolves had to plow along, chest deep, in the soft stuff. If the snow had been crusted, their oversize feet would have acted as snowshoes and held them up, but in the soft, deep piles left by the storm they had to struggle along by brute force.

Big Black led them downstream along the canyon in which they had spent the night. Where the ravine opened onto a larger canyon he swung onto a frozen river which meandered between the hills. By now the sun had risen and was casting long, black shadows of bare willows and birch across the snow. The morning was very cold and as the wolves plowed along, clouds of their frozen breath shrouded them. A squirrel chattered down from his station on a pine bough. The wolves stopped and looked up. They were extremely curious animals, always aware of what was happening around them. Stay alert or die. It was a basic law in the unforgiving world in which they lived. And it applied to all wildlife. If you were a mouse, a strange noise might mean a snake or an owl or a weasel or any one of the hundred predators which hunted you; if you were a deer, it might be a wolf that was closing in; if you were a wolf, it could be that most deadly of all enemies—man. So stay alert.

The pack's trail followed the river out of the hills and onto a meadow where, in summer, moose fed on the watercress and willow shoots. As Lupus followed along in file behind Big Black, he spotted something hanging in a clump of grass a few yards away from the trail. He broke out of line and bounded awkwardly through the deep snow toward the object. The pup had seen the owl's feather, lost by the bird in the morning's dark hours. He pushed his way up to it and stood, head cocked, studying the feather and the delicate imprint of the owl's wings in the soft snow. He nuzzled into the snow. He flopped onto his side and rolled back and forth over the spot, twisting and turning as though to cover his body with the intriguing scents left by the owl and rodent. Then he stood and vigorously shook the snow from his fur. After marking the clump of grass he bounded back to the trail after his pack, which was now far downstream.

Later that morning another wolf found Lupus' scent post. He was a lean, rangy male with battle-scarred muzzle and ears, a straggler from the wolf pack which lived farther west in the forest. His fur was torn from one shoulder, the result of a recent fight. The wolf had lost his mate during the previous breeding season; instead of becoming the kindly old uncle of the pack, as often happened in such cases, he had turned mean, fighting with the other wolves until they drove him away. Now he was a loner drifting through the forest.

The Loner had been moving downstream when he discovered the pack's trail. On the meadow he turned aside to investigate the churned-up snow where Lupus had found the owl's feather. He nosed Lupus' scent post and added his own mark. Then, nose down, he followed the pup's scent back to the trail. He caught up with the pack a mile downstream.

The wolves were sitting on a bluff overlooking the river. Below them a bull moose was browsing among the willows, unaware of the hungry wolves above him. When he was directly below the pack they tensed, ready to bound down on him. At that moment the Loner trotted into view. He saw the moose and broke into a gallop. The bull heard him, looked up, and broke out of the willows. Big Black, intent on watching the moose, was unaware of the Loner. When the moose burst from the thicket, Big Black and the rest of the pack took after him. All but Lupus. He *had* seen the Loner and he dashed out at him, for strange wolves were not tolerated in the pack's territory. The pup smashed at full speed into the surprised Loner. Now the many weeks of rough-and-tumble play paid off. Before the strange wolf could regain his feet Lupus was slashing at him. The Loner broke free and crouched, ears back and teeth bared. But he was beaten and he knew it. In the first place, he was in another pack's territory and this gave Lupus an immediate advantage. Also, he was weak from both hunger and the many beatings he had already taken from the members of his own pack. He backed away. Lupus attacked again. The Loner snapped and caught the pup's lip, drawing blood. But Lupus tore loose and grabbed the stranger's throat. Over and over they rolled in the snow. The Loner broke free and ran, his tail between his legs. At the head of the meadow he left the trail and bounded toward the shelter of the forest. Lupus stood watching him. The old wolf retreated among the trees and was never seen again in Big Black's territory.

Lupus galloped down the trail. His pack had brought the moose to bay in a clump of willows. The moose was a mature bull, four years old and in his prime, with sixty-pound "palmated" antlers, so-called because of the webbing between their tines. He was big even for a moose, which is the largest member of the deer family, and he weighed more than eighteen hundred pounds. The dewlap of hair, called a "bell," hanging from his throat waved back and forth when the moose swung his head to face first one, then another of the wolves.

After the initial panic caused by the sudden appearance of the Loner, the moose had stopped running and turned to face the pack. He stood panting and spraddle-legged, watching the wolves who fanned out in front of him. From time to time one dashed in to attack. The moose snorted and cut the air with a swing of his massive antlers. Had he caught the wolf he would have disemboweled it. But the wolves were wise in the behavior of besieged moose; they kept their distance. After ten minutes they had had enough of the stalemate. They moved back onto the trail and the moose returned to his morning's browsing.

Later the pack raised another moose, one which wasn't wise enough to stand his ground. He took off at an awkward trot with the wolves strung out single file behind. But he easily outdistanced them as they floundered along in the deep snow, and after a quarter mile chase they gave up.

Hunting is a serious business for the wolves. They do not set out to bag a moose or deer for sport as a human hunter might. The wolves hunt in order to live; it is that simple. And contrary to myths about them, wolves are not bloodthirsty killers, slashing with their fangs just to spill blood whenever and wherever they can. They take just enough to satisfy their hunger, and for a pack of eleven animals that means that one average-sized moose must be killed each four or five days. This can be a dangerous task. Moose can weigh more than twelve times as much as the wolves and often the hunt is unsuccessful. According to Dr. L. David Mech, a wolf pack must attack about thirteen moose before it kills one of them. Hunting is hard, dangerous work for wolves.

Yet they *must* hunt. So, late in the afternoon of that cold January day the pack moved out for another attempt to find food. They raised an old cow moose along the edge of a lake.

The cow was browsing on poplar trees, stretching her neck far among the branches and stripping away the twigs. If the wolves had jumped her a few years earlier with a calf at her side, the results of their hunt might have been much different. Now the cow was old, well beyond her fertile years. Her teeth were worn down to the gumline, making feeding difficult; so she was undernourished. She was further weakened by several large tapeworm cysts which incubated inside her lungs.

But the instinct for self-preservation beats hard in even the oldest, sickest animals; when the moose heard the pack coming at her, she ran. This time the wolves were not to be denied. They snapped at the moose's hindquarters and sliced long wounds in her flanks. She stopped running and turned to face her tormentors. The wolves drew back and sat on the snow waiting for her to weaken. She tried to run; the pack cut her off. She fell to her knees. The wolves advanced. The moose struggled upright; the wolves retreated. They knew that the battle was theirs. The moose stood quietly for a few minutes then slumped to the snow. The pack moved in and finished her.

The cow was old and diseased, of no further use to the moose population of the forest. She could no longer bear calves, and she ate food needed by healthy, young moose. In the wilderness an individual animal is valuable only so long as it is healthy and able to bear babies or, if it is a male, to sire and protect them. When it grows old or ill it is tossed aside to die of starvation or to be killed by predators. And because the predators take these rejects far more often than healthy adults, they are vital to the overall balance of nature. (We must make an exception of man's predation, for all too often he slaughters entire species, a thing which other predators never do.)

When the wolves ate the moose carcass they also consumed the tapeworm cysts which were attached to the cow's lungs. These cysts were sacs enclosing the larvae of the tapeworms. The cysts were ruptured by the wolves' teeth and the larvae passed into the animals' intestines. There, they developed into adult tapeworms which attached themselves to the intestinal walls and stole food from the wolves. When the worms matured they laid eggs which were passed out with the wolves' waste. The eggs fell onto the grass and were eaten by grazing moose and deer. They hatched into larvae and moved through their hosts' bloodstreams until they reached the lungs where they encysted, completing the cycle.

This complicated relationship between the tapeworm and the animals on which it depends is an example of an ecological relationship. *Ecology* is the science which studies the manner in which all forms of life relate to each other.

The wolves are essential parts of the tapeworm's life cycle, yet are not weakened by the adult tapeworms as the moose are by the cysts. Scientists who have studied the matter think that over the thousands of years that wild wolves have played their roles in the little drama, they have developed an immunity to the parasites they carry around in their intestines.

February came to Superior National Forest. Snow continued to fall and the temperature stayed well below freezing during those last weeks of winter. The wolves of Big Black's pack were constantly on the move as they scouted for food. When they made a kill they gorged themselves; when they missed, as they often did, they went hungry. They rested after each meal and traveled many miles to find the next.

Lupus had grown hard and strong. His body had filled out and his legs had developed the long, powerful muscles that carried him at a jogging trot for miles without rest. The

A mature gray wolf.

GEORGE WILSON

keen instincts of the hunter with which he had been born ripened and became as much a part of his daily life as his sight and hearing. With each hunt he learned something new about his craft and he remembered what he had learned. His puppyhood lay far behind in the forest's gentler seasons. He was an adult wolf in all ways except one—sexual maturity. It would be another year before he mated.

So the changes which crept into the pack's behavior in mid-February did little except confuse him. They were very subtle changes at first, ever-so-slight differences in the way in which the adults behaved. Tempers were a bit shorter; hackles came up more often; fangs were bared ever so slightly; growls were heard. The female wolves grew flirtatious. Muzzle nipping and shoulder bumping became something more than the greeting of friends. Males became nervous if other males moved too close to certain females. Big Black asserted his dominance more frequently and with a bit less restraint. The normal, relaxed friendliness of the pack slipped bit by bit away to be replaced by a tension which seemed to crackle from wolf to wolf. The breeding season was approaching.

In most ways wolves and dogs are very much alike. Their common ancestry has given them similar physical characteristics. Both are carnivores and hunters, despite the fact that man has bred much of this hunting instinct out of many domestic breeds. Wolves and dogs can interbreed and produce fertile young. But there is one area where they differ markedly, and that is in their breeding patterns. Dogs can and do mate at any time of the year. Wolves have a single mating season about six weeks long, from mid-February to April. At all other times the breeding instinct is either absent or so reduced as to be unapparent. Why should two such similar groups within the same family differ so much in this one area of their lives? Probably, the answer has to do with the wolves' totally wild nature. Unlike dogs, they have never been truly domesticated.

Nature, that harsh lawgiver, discloses one of her gentler sides in the care she provides her wild babies. She usually schedules their arrival in the world for the moment when they have the best chance of survival. In most instances this is in the spring for animals of the earth's temperate and polar regions. Babies born then will have all summer and autumn in which to grow and learn before they have to face the cold, barren winter.

But we must be careful in thinking that this truly demonstrates a gentleness in nature or some magical wisdom to determine the best time for babies to be born. The real magic is in each species' ability to adapt to its environment and to pass that adaptation along to the following generations, for this is what actually decided the matter. Once upon a time, maybe millions of years ago, babies might have come at any season of the year. Those born in the spring survived to have babies of their own; those which appeared at other times, did not. So a gradual genetic change took place. Today, the genes, which dictate that an undeveloped egg will be a wolf or a moose or whatever, also order mature animals to mate only when the resulting babies will be born at the best possible time.

By the first of March the wolves were feeling the full impact of this drive. The pack still hunted, of course, but when the wolves were not on the trail there was much nervous milling around between them. The one dependable feature of pack life—the "glue" which held it together during these trying times—was its strict social pattern, the position of each wolf inherited through genes and won or lost by fangs while the animal was growing. As explained before, each wolf was either dominant over or submissive to others in the pack. Only Big Black was dominant over all; only Flop Ear was totally submissive. Between these extreme positions relationships among the wolves were complex and confusing. The conflict of strict social order colliding with the urgent drive to mate produced several turbulent weeks.

Big Black desired Lupus' mother. But she had eyes for another male, one slightly lower on the social ladder than Big Black. That male, however, wanted still another female. But Lupus' mother was the other female's superior and drove her away whenever the male was near. The other members of the pack had equally complicated desires. Jealousies developed into actual fighting. Poor Big Black, who because of his position as leader was also policeman, judge, and jury, had to dash back and forth, separating the snarling wolves. He carried his tail in the dominant, erect position and any wolf who tried to stand up to him faced a sound thrashing. But Big Black was as driven by the desire to mate as any other member of the pack, and between courting Lupus' mother and keeping the peace he was a very busy wolf indeed. The two-year-old pups tried to find mates, but they were so young and so far down the social scale that their efforts were in vain.

However, relatively few other members of the pack had any more success. Too much time and energy were spent chasing away rivals and courting to leave enough for actual mating. Once, while Big Black was breaking up a fight, Lupus' mother chased off the rival for her chosen male and mated with him. Hers would be one of the two litters born to the pack the following spring, and although Big Black was not their father he would accept and care for the pups as though they were his own. To Lupus, the entire breeding season was a puzzle and he sat aside while the adults courted. A vague desire, a full year from its final flowering, sent him near a female once but her suitor dashed in and drove the pup away. He really didn't care too much since he didn't know what it all was about anyway. So he sat scratching while the others ran here and there, busy in their need to produce pups.

By the end of March it was all over. The tensions and jealousies disappeared. Wolves who had been deadly rivals just a few days earlier now slept peacefully side by side. No grudges were held. It was done for another year and the pack was once more a group of close friends hunting, eating, and living together. They drifted toward Den Hill, where Lupus had been born almost a year earlier and where next spring's litters would be whelped.

Winter was dying. On the southern slopes of the forest, where the sun shone most of each day, bare ground peeked through the snow. Rivulets of water trickled down the little ravines and canyons and out onto the lakes, melting the snow which still lay on the frozen surfaces. At night this water froze again and the lakes were glazed by sheets of glare ice—smooth, slippery, and very dangerous to any animal which ventured onto it. It was impossible to walk on without falling and any deer which went down stayed down, unable to get a foothold. The wolf pack knew about glare ice and avoided it whenever possible.

They traveled early in the mornings now, while the snow in the forest was still crusted from the previous night's freeze and before the day's melting turned it to slush. They returned to the access road where Lupus had made his first, serious chase of a deer. They passed the spot where a black bear had frightened the pups when they and Old Uncle had left the main pack for a few weeks. The bear was still asleep in a cave. Two one-pound cubs born during the winter crawled over her. If their wintry birth might seem to violate nature's practice of having her babies appear at the time best suited for their survival, remember that the cubs were born in a warm cave and had their mother's furry body to shelter them while storms still raged above ground. When they finally emerged in spring, they would be large enough to trail after their mother as she foraged through the forest. Had they been born a few weeks later than they actually were, the mother bear would have had to leave them unprotected while she searched for the food she needed after her long sleep.

The wolves crossed the little canyon where Lupus had killed his first beaver. Here, protected from the sun, winter still held on. Deep snow covered the ground and the wolves had to fight their way through the drifts. They crossed Pine Tree Meadow and the stream where Lupus had watched the otters playing. Finally in late March they came to the den site. The meadow at its base was brown and drab in the early spring sun. Four white birches stood on Den Hill. A fifth, the victim of the storm which had killed one of the pups, lay across the ruins of last year's den. The fallen pine tree which had caused the flooding of Den Hill was gone, swept away by the heavy runoff of snow water, and the hill was warm and dry, drained by the little ravine which bordered it.

The pregnant wolves began to work on their dens. Lupus' mother dug a new one, well away from the birches. The other mother-to-be cleaned out one of the old dens, then dug another under the fallen birch.

Lupus and the rest of the pack settled down for the stay at Den Hill. A full year had passed since the pack's last visit. It had been a normal year, filled with the usual activity and hazards. Of the six pups born the previous spring, only two still lived—Lupus and his sister Flop Ear, the underdog. This was normal, in fact, better than the average survival of pups, for during their first year wolf young, as most wild babies, suffer an extremely high mortality rate. The pack had lost one adult, Old Uncle; this also was not unusual. A pack normally has one or more old individuals trailing along with it who eventually die. The wolves had had few contacts with men, and this was good. Of all the dangers the pack faced, the two-legged killers were the greatest threat to their safety.

By mid-March when winter formally gave way to spring the first, faint hint of green showed among the willows which lined the little stream in the meadow. The pack lay on Den Hill, soaking in the warmth, scratching fleas, content to be alive. One evening, shortly after their arrival, they gathered for a songfest. Heads were thrown back, tails were raised to whatever level the individual's rank in the pack allowed. Shoulders were bumped, muzzles nipped, eyes closed and the first notes of the wolves' wild, free call echoed among the trees. Lupus stood with the others, singing in a clear, powerful voice.

He was one year old, a fully grown wolf. He weighed more than one hundred pounds, larger than most wolves of the forest. He had a strong, hard body overlaid with powerful muscles. His coat, somewhat straggly looking now with the molting of its winter's undercoat, was rich and full, black and white with traces of rust. His almond-shaped, golden eyes were clear and alert. The tuft of black hair which

Howling.   GEORGE WILSON

bridged his muzzle gave him a dignified, an almost arrogant, appearance. His tail was full, a beautiful brush of gray hair with a tuft of pure black at its tip. He had all the hunting tools he needed—strength; keen eyes and ears; long, white teeth; a massive chest for endurance; powerful legs that could carry him for miles without stopping. And in the one year of his life he had grown wise in the ways of the forest; he knew which animals he must hunt and which he must avoid in order to live.

Lupus was the product of one hundred thousand generations of wolves. They had passed on to him the very best they had—courage, intelligence, strength. Unless he met with an accident or disease took him, and unless he fell to man's guns or traps or poison, he would live for ten to sixteen years. After Big Black died he probably would be the pack's leader.

But that was years away. For now the spring sun was warm and good friends were gathered together for a songfest. Afterward, there was the hunt.

Part III
Fables and Facts

The gray wolf, a most misunderstood animal.

GEORGE WILSON

There is a well-known fable about a wolf who wanted to get at a flock of sheep, but each time he appeared the sheep bleated in terror, bringing their shepherd who drove the wolf away. So the wily creature draped himself with a sheepskin. Then when the flock saw him they assumed he was simply another sheep and allowed him to move in and kill them.

Aesop is supposed to have written this story in the sixth century B.C. A few hundred years later one of the authors of the Bible wrote, "Beware of false prophets which come to you in sheep's clothing, but inward they are ravening wolves." Today we label an enemy who poses as a friend "a wolf in sheep's clothing."

This story actually goes back at least five hundred years before Aesop's time. Who knows when and where it really started? It is just one of many which man has invented about wolves and, as in most of them, the wolf is cast as a villain. He appears over and over again in our fairy tales—"Little Red Riding Hood," "The Three Little Pigs," "Peter and the Wolf," "The Boy Who Cried Wolf." There is one story which comes from Russia. In it, a nobleman (or lady, according to the whim of the storyteller) is riding with his family in a horse-drawn sled, a *troika*. Deep in a forest they are pursued by a pack of howling wolves intent on killing them. From this point the story has several versions. In one of the more grisly, the nobleman throws his babies to the wolves, one by one; while the bloodthirsty pack attacks the helpless infants, the rest of the family escapes.

Out of all the legends about wolves a long list of sayings has developed. "Beware of the wolf in sheep's clothing" is one; here is the gist of a few others:

"To cry wolf" means to give a false alarm of danger.

"To keep the wolf from the door" is to ward off starvation.

"To throw to the wolves" is to sacrifice someone for one's own safety or well-being.

"To put your head in the wolf's mouth" is to needlessly expose yourself to danger. Another saying, "Putting your head in the lion's mouth," implies the same foolhardiness.

"To be as hungry as a wolf" is to be ravenous.

"To wolf your food" is to eat rapidly.

"To hold a wolf by the ears" is to be in a situation in which it is as dangerous to let go as to hold on. "Having a tiger by the tail" is another way of stating the same unfortunate condition.

If a man is called a wolf today it means that he is a ladies' man, very fond of the girls. But at one time a person known as a wolf was considered to be mean, inhuman, a killer. Still earlier, probably beginning in ancient Greece, some people were thought to actually become wolves and to prey on other humans. These demented souls—actually insane people— were called werewolves and often were buried alive, a practice especially common in the Middle Ages in Europe.

What do these sayings and many others of a similar nature imply? In the first place and by their very numbers they indicate that man has had a long, close association with wolves. Stanley P. Young and Edward A. Goldman wrote in their book *The Wolves of North America* that the gray wolf has been more important to man than any other hunting animal and that it had a range that probably was larger than any other land mammal. As we might expect, this combination of large numbers and great range brought it into contact with most of the people on earth. And after man became civilized, "contact" usually meant "conflict."

A second thing that most wolf fables rather strongly suggest is that man, white man especially, does not have a very high regard for wolves. At best he sees them as gluttonous, voracious and bad mannered. At worst he considers them to be bloodthirsty, vicious, cunning, and wanton killers whose entire lives are one continuous orgy of slaughter.

Wolves are just one of nature's many predators yet they carry the bulk of man's wrath. Lions, for instance, also hunt other animals but they are assumed by man to have far nobler virtues; we hear expressions like "the noble lion," "king of the jungle," etc. Why are wolves so often cast as villains?

To begin with, they are very efficient predators, a fact which man finds troublesome. They learned long ago to overcome the disadvantages which evolution gave them—a relatively small size and the lack of talons. They organized into packs for better hunting. They developed a keen intelligence. One authority claims that wolves are to the Canids what man is to the Primates. That is, wolves stand at the head of the dog family just as man stands at the head of his.

Man began his existence as a hunter, a predator very much like wolves. He too had serious disadvantages to overcome—smallness, weakness, the lack of natural weapons. He made up for them by developing and using his brain. He learned to hold a club or rock which he swung or threw at his prey. At some point in his development he figured out what the wolves had learned long before, that an excellent way to overcome many of his disadvantages was to live with other men—to form a pack for defending his territory and for better hunting. Today we know this pack as the family and nation; man's territory is his home and country.

So long as man remained a hunter, he and the wolves got along rather well together. Even today among primitive people who hunt for a living there is no animosity toward wolves. Each species learned very early that it faced real hazards in attacking the other. Both were concerned with hunting for food with as little effort and danger as possible, and it was far better to go after animals that didn't fight back. The more easily one could get his food, the more time and energy he had left for other activities.

Man learned this lesson well, and about nine thousand years ago in Asia Minor he invented a food gathering process which forever changed his relationship with wolves. He discovered that he could get more food far more easily by domesticating certain animals than by hunting them. What he invented was the science of animal husbandry. Man the hunter became man the herder.

It was one thing for man the hunter to live side by side with wolves as each went about his business stalking the rich supply of game animals which lived then. It was quite another matter for man the herder to allow wolves access to his cattle and sheep, even though by killing off game animals which the wolves needed he was partially responsible for the raids.

Man declared war—the Great Wolf War—and set about to exterminate these "vermin," as he called the wolves. He dug pits for them to fall in and set steel traps which broke their legs. He used guns which shot them when they took a bait and deadfalls which crashed down to break their backs. He burned them alive by setting fire to the forests in which they lived and poisoned them with strychnine, a substance which causes prolonged, agonizing death. (When the Great Wolf War was at its height in America, an unwritten law demanded that each range rider carry strychnine to put in animal carcasses he found in order to kill the wolves which came to eat them.) Special breeds of dogs, such as the Irish wolfhound, were developed to kill wolves. Many people were enlisted in the war—farmers, ranchers, soldiers, and bounty hunters who were paid for each wolf they killed. (In North America alone, more than *one hundred million dollars* has been spent in bounties, much of it to control wolves.) In 1915 the United States Government established the Bureau of Biological Control, which hired professional hunters to go out after the wolves. In Russia almost one hundred thousand poisoned baits were used in just one of the nation's republics. In Sweden the Lapp herders are allowed to kill wolves on sight, even in national parks.

The Great Wolf War has been long and costly. It has also been successful. Wolves were exterminated from England by the beginning of the sixteenth century and from Ireland by the end of the seventeenth. They were gone from Scotland by the middle of the eighteenth century and from France by the end of World War I. In the United States there were no wolves east of the Mississippi, except for northern Wisconsin and Michigan, by 1940.

Now the battle is about finished, at least in the western hemisphere; the wolves have lost. From two million when the white men came, their numbers have slipped to a few thousand—a handful in the continental United States with the rest scattered throughout Canada and Alaska.

Was the war really needed?

Where wolves posed a real threat to man's herds they had to be controlled. For instance, they could not be allowed to destroy half of one year's crop of calves as they did during the nineteenth century in Texas. But that does not justify the extermination of an entire species. And now that man's livestock is safe what excuse is there to continue the Great War?

Some people argue that wolves pose a threat to human life, and it is true that there were attacks against people many years ago in Europe. But at least one wolf authority argues that there were three good reasons for them. In the first place, Europe is quite small and as its human population increased there were many contacts with wolves; attacks were inevitable. Secondly, there is good evidence that the attacks were made by rabid wolves. We know that any animal having rabies—a wolf, a skunk, or even a cow—will attack humans and other animals. Finally, from available records it appears that most of the wolves which attacked Europeans were not true wolves at all. They were hybrids, the offspring of matings between wolves and dogs. Such animals tend to be vicious.

Assuming that these explanations account for wolf attacks on people in Europe, how do we explain supposed assaults in North America? The answer is simple. There have been very few, if any. Rutter and Pimlott state in their book *The World of the Wolf* that there is no evidence that wolves have ever posed a threat to man in North America. An experiment conducted by a newspaper editor in Canada seems to bear this out. He offered a reward to anyone who could prove an unprovoked wolf attack on a human. Although the reward stood for several years it was never claimed.

So why do the bloody myths hang on today? The vast majority of civilized people have never even seen a wild wolf. Why does the old hatred persist?

One reason might be that it *is* so old. Hatred of wolves goes back to the days of the herdsmen; it has become part of human tradition. And any tradition is extremely difficult to change. For instance, many people believe that a person can catch a cold by sitting in a draft. Nonsense. *If* that person already has a supply of cold viruses in his system, and *if* his resistance to them already is low, the draft can reduce his body temperature just enough to allow them to take over. But a normal, healthy human does not catch cold merely by being exposed to a draft. Yet year after year millions of mothers around the world warn their children to "Get out of that draft; you'll catch cold."

The wolf is like the misunderstood draft. To hundreds of generations of children he has been the drooling monster who lies in wait for Little Red Riding Hood or who blows the foolish Little Pigs' houses down. He is the villain of movie cartoons and television ads. He has slipped into our folklore as evil, and we don't bother to find out what is truth and what is fable.

There is one group of people who hate wolves and who should know better. These are the "sportsmen," hunters who go out after deer, elk, moose, and the other game animals. They argue that wolves destroy the big game population. This is not true. In the first place, it would violate one of nature's fundamental laws: A predator species absolutely may not overkill its prey. If such a thing happened the predator would be killing off the source of its own food and in short order would starve. Natural predators and their prey have been living together for millions of years, each balancing the other's numbers. If there is a population explosion of ground squirrels in a given year, there will be a corresponding increase in the number of predators that prey on them. And if the ground squirrels decrease because of disease or drought, the population of the predators will sag. This is how the ecological balances operate unless man interferes. His heavy hand can be disastrous, as the episode of the Kaibab deer so dramatically demonstrated.

But the "sportsmen" are right in one respect: The population of deer is decreasing in certain areas. If natural predators are not responsible, what is? Here is one explanation: During the early days of the United States men cut millions of acres of trees. Much of this was to clear farmland, and after the trees were cut the land was cultivated. But many thousands of acres were cut for timber and where this happened the land was allowed to remain fallow. Stripped of trees and open to the sun it grew a cover of grass, brush, and saplings—ideal deer fodder. The deer population exploded much to the delight of hunters. But this condition lasted only until second-growth forest reclaimed the cleared areas. Then, with their food supply cut back, the deer's numbers fell. So, by felling enormous sections of the forests, men created an artificially large deer population. By allowing the trees to grow back they were responsible for reducing that population. Wolves and other natural predators had nothing to do with it.

Hunters also claim that wolves are reducing the caribou herds of Alaska and northern Canada. These two species have lived side by side for much longer than man has been in America, yet it is true that the number of caribou is falling. Why?

Earlier in this book I suggested that of all predators, only man hunts in a destructive manner. The others take what they need in order to live. Man has freed himself of the necessity to hunt for his living and now does it for sport, for recreation. But whether he hunts for the food he needs or for a fine trophy head to hang on his wall, when man kills wild animals he is as much a predator as wolves and he must obey nature's law that a predator may not kill more of his prey than that species is capable of replacing through reproduction. Man often disregards this law. This is what is happening to the caribou; man, specifically the "sportsman," is killing too many of them.

Farley Mowat in his book *Never Cry Wolf* describes an incident which, unfortunately, takes place all too often. While he lived in the Arctic, Mr. Mowat tried to convince people that wolves were not villains. But the people would not listen. (Old traditions die hard. Remember?) One day a trader claimed he had proof that a pack of wolves had slaughtered a caribou herd just for fun and had left the meat to rot. Mr. Mowat visited the place where the massacre supposedly happened. Sure enough, there on the ice of a frozen lake lay the bodies of twenty-three caribou, all but three untouched. Two of these three were bucks whose heads had been cut off; the third was a pregnant doe whose hindquarters were gone. But there were no wolf tracks, only the ski trails of an airplane which had landed and taxied around the lake. The caribou had not been killed by wolves; they had been shot by "sportsmen" flown in by the plane. Apparently, when the pilot spotted the caribou herd he landed and rounded up the animals by taxiing around them on the lake while his passengers shot them from the plane's doors and windows. After the caribou were dead the "sportsmen" stepped out of the plane and cut off the two best trophy heads. The tender hindquarters of the pregnant doe were taken for meat.

Bloodthirsty *wolves?*

The old legends are lies, hand-me-downs from a time when man was a primitive herder, protecting his livestock from the creatures of the wilderness. They have no place in today's world. It is time to take a fresh look at wolves and at all wildlife. If we do not, the moment will come—perhaps in your lifetime, surely in your children's—when there will be no wild animals living in the wilderness. In fact, there will be no wilderness for them to live in.

This raises the question, "So what?"

What difference will it make if every wild wolf and deer, every mountain lion and antelope, every forest and swamp disappear from the earth? After all, man now is a creature of the city and eventually the vast majority of us will live in houses set on paved streets. Even now, most people in "civilized" countries never experience the wilderness. How many have heard an eagle scream or a quail call to its babies? How many have seen the seasons follow each other in some corner of the forest where man is merely a visitor?

At some point in time man chose to become civilized. There was nothing wrong with this decision. Because of it you and I can live fairly comfortable lives. We do not have to carry water from a well nor hunt for our food. Snug in our houses we are reasonably safe from winter's cold and summer's heat. We eat food bought at a grocery, drink water purified and piped to us by elaborate supply systems, wear ready-made clothing. We watch television, listen to the radio, talk over great distances on the telephone, drive automobiles. Man has raised dams, built great cities, reached the moon, and is headed for the other planets. We are the masters of the universe.

Or are we?

Every day we are reminded of the high price we pay for the products of civilization. The air in our large cities is unfit to breathe because of the exhaust from cars and factories; the waters of our rivers, our lakes, and the ocean itself are polluted by human sewage, pesticides, and the waste from industry; our food contains fallout from H-bomb tests and the poisonous chemicals we dump on our farmlands; the noise in our cities rises to a deafening roar from ever-larger trucks and jet planes; our countryside is becoming a graveyard of litter.

We are beginning to realize that this cannot continue, that we must protect our natural environment if we are not to smother in our own filth. Strange as it might seem, wild animals can help us do this. Scientists tell us that we can learn much from them. We can use them to help conquer disease, to study the origins of life, to learn more about human behavior, to investigate the effects of pollution and noise. There is a steady flow of new information coming from scientific laboratories and much of it raises still other questions which wild animals can help answer.

There is another area, one not so readily studied by science, which is vital to human welfare. Here, too, the animals can be great teachers.

It seems to me that the single greatest mistake man made while becoming civilized was to assume, simply because he was capable of inventing powerful machines and building great cities, that he was the master of nature. He thought that he could contaminate the natural environment without having to pay for his thoughtlessness. He set himself aside from the rest of the universe as a special being who was not subject to nature's laws. This is nonsense. *All living things are merely parts of nature; none, including man, is its master.*

The animals, especially wild animals, know this instinctively because they still live so very close to nature. They can teach us this truth if we will let them. They can remind us that all living creatures share a magnificent journey which began two billion years ago when life appeared on earth. Regardless of the countless different paths we took as we spread out to fill our own special niches on the earth, we are all parts of one family. And we need each other. Sometimes that need is direct and can be defined by scientists, such as the tapeworm's need for its moose and wolf hosts. But at other times it is much more subtle and defies description. For instance, how can anyone possibly describe the need which is fulfilled by watching a pair of birds build their nest or by listening to a squirrel chatter in a tree. But simply because we cannot speak of these things does not mean they are any less important to our well-being. Think of how poor we would be if the wonders of nature were taken away. What a sad, lonely world. Man would be alone, without the rest of his family.

By studying the wild, free lives of animals, directly or from films or books, we learn a respect for nature. We gain a real appreciation of the way that all things—air, soil, water, and the living creatures—fit together as pieces in a living jigsaw puzzle. And any person who appreciates nature in this way comes to realize a most important fact: *All* life is important and necessary if the puzzle is to be complete.

When we discover this truth perhaps we will not exterminate the other members of our family. And maybe we will leave wilderness areas for them to live in. We will not destroy *all* the forests, or drain *all* the swamps, or build roads through *all* the wild places. You and your children will not be robbed of what is rightfully yours and theirs—a world that is fit to live in. There will be clean air and water and a wealth of wild animals to be enjoyed.

And if we truly learn to live with nature and not merely to exploit it and its creatures, some day, if you are very lucky, you might even hear wild wolves singing. On a warm afternoon deep in the northern woods or on the barren lands of the far north as you sit resting from a hike through the free, untouched wilderness, you might hear it.

Across a hill or deep among the trees, the pack will gather

around its leader. There will be friendly milling around; furry shoulders will be bumped, muzzles nipped, tails wagged. Heads will be thrown back and golden, almond-shaped eyes shut. One of the wolves will start the singing. His voice will be low and full. The rest of the pack will join in, some as deep, full-throated bassos and others as sopranos who send their voices climbing to swoop and soar over the chorus. Some will sing in shimmering tremulos and others will "mouth" their voices. The howling will carry for miles in the warm afternoon air. It will fade, then perhaps be picked up by one of the wolves and started all over again. Finally it will die and the wilderness will lie quiet. The wolves will move out to hunt; you will be alone, filled and rich with the memory of what many people call the most beautiful sound in the wilderness.

In Appreciation

Man has lived side by side with wolves for thousands of years, yet he has only recently studied them scientifically. Scientific studies have shown that the old myths about wolves are, for the most part, false. These scientific findings provided the material for this book. Although the story of Lupus the wolf pup is fiction, it is plausible fiction; that is, if it didn't happen it could have, for it is based on field studies of wolves. Not my studies—I am merely a storyteller—but the work of such scientists as Stanley P. Young, Edward A. Goldman, and Dr. Adolph Murie, all pioneers in the scientific field study of wolves; of Dr. L. David Mech, who worked with the wolves of Isle Royale; and of Russell J. Rutter and Douglas H. Pimlott, who worked together on the wolves of eastern Canada. I owe much to those naturalists who lived in the wilderness for long periods studying wild wolves; the two who come most readily to mind in this category are Lois Crisler and Farley Mowat. Finally, I am grateful to my friend George Wilson and his friend Homer the wolf, who was the model for Lupus.

To all of these and countless other dedicated scientists, naturalists, and conservationists whose work helps the cause of wild animals and the wild places they need, I say thank you.

Further Reading

There are many fine books about wolves. Here are a few which you might enjoy reading.

Caras, Roger, *The Custer Wolf*, Boston, Little, Brown and Co., 1966.
   The story of a renegade wolf in South Dakota who for years outwitted the hunters who sought him in the early part of the twentieth century.
Crisler, Lois, *Arctic Wild*, New York, Harper and Row, 1958.
   The story of the year which the author and her husband spent in the Brooks Range in Alaska and of the wild wolves who came to live with them.
Mech, L. David, "The Wolves of Isle Royale," *Fauna of the National Parks of the United States, Series 7,* Washington, D.C., U.S. Government Printing Office, 1966.
   The scientific results of Dr. Mech's study of the pack of wild wolves living in Isle Royale National Park.
Mowat, Farley, *Never Cry Wolf,* Boston, Little, Brown and Co., 1963.
   The story of the author's experience as a field biologist studying the wolves of the far north for the Canadian government.
Murie, Adolph, *A Naturalist in Alaska,* New York, Devin-Adair Co., 1961.
   A story of the author's ramblings through Alaska.

Rutter, Russell J. and Pimlott, Douglas H., *The World of the Wolf*, Philadelphia, J. B. Lippincott & Company, 1967.
The story of the authors' observations of the wolves of Algonquin National Park in Ontario, Canada.

Young, Stanley P. and Goldman, Edward A., *The Wolves of North America*, Vols. I and II, New York, 1964.
The results of the authors' lengthy study of the wolves in North America from the time that white men first came to the continent.

Index

Samoyeds, 10
Scotland and wolf extermination, 120
Seals, 6
Senses, 62–63, *63*, 76–77
Settlers, 25–26; effects of, 25–26
  enemies of, 3–4
  livestock of, 3–4, 15, 22
  (*see also* Ranchers)
Sexual maturity, 106–109
Skunks, 75, 76
Sloths, ground, 11
Smell, 77
Snow, 85, 92–93, *98*
Songfests, 58–61, 68, 111–113, *112*
South America, maned wolf of, *8*, 9
Sportsmen: and aerial hunting, 124
  overkill by, 122–124
Squirrels, 75, 79
Storms, 47–50, 65–66, 92–93
Superior National Forest, 30, 52, 74,
  75, 81, 104
Sweden and wolf extermination, 120

Tapeworms, 103–104
Tasmania, pouched wolf of, *9*, 9–10
Teeth, 77
Temperature, 92–93
Tigers, sabre-toothed, 11
Timber, 123
Trot, 69, *82*

United States: Bureau of Biological
  Control, 120
  Forest Service, 69
  and wolf extermination, 120

Vermin, 26, 119–120
Vision, 76–77

Walk, 70
Wapiti, *19*
Weasels, 6, 11
Werewolves, 117
Whelping season, 34–37
Wilson, George, 115, 129
Winter preparations, 79
Wolf naps, 92
Wolf packs: authority in, 86–89
  calling of, 83
  hunting by, 14–22, 23–24, 68–73
  hunting routes of, 74–75
  social structure of, 30–31
  songfests of, 58–61, *59, 60*, 68, 111–
  113, *112*

trails of, 97–104
  (*see also* Wolves, gray)
Wolves: aardwolf, *8*, 9
  dire, 10–11
  Eurasian, 3
  evolution of, 3–26
  maned, *8*, 9
  pouched, *9*, 9–10
  red, 10, 12
Wolves, gray, *105, 114*
  alertness of, 99
  birth of, 34–36, *35*
  and bison, 5
  coats of, *95*
  dens of, 31–34, *32*, 110
  description of, 12, 13, 111–113
  efficiency of, 118
  extermination of, 26, 119–120
  fangs of, *71*
  gaits of, 69
  gestation of, 28–30
  growth of, 53–73, 77–78
  hearing of, 77
  hunting instinct of, 53, 61–65
  hybridization of, 10
  instincts of, 56
  intelligence of, 118
  legends about, 21–22, 25, 116–118
  litters of, 31–51
  mating of, 106–109
  organization of, 118
  pelts of, 23
  populations of, 117
  prejudices against, 115–128
  pups of, 28–51, 36–51, *35, 45, 50,*
  54, 57, 63, 67–73
  range of, 3–5, 10, 117
  sayings about, 116–117
  sense of smell of, 77
  skins of, 23
  social organization of, 88–89, 107–
  108
  socializing of, 61
  tail-crossing of, *87*
  teeth of, 77
  trot of, *82*
  vision of, 76–77
  weaning of, 51
  (*see also* Wolf packs)
Wolves of North America, The, 117
Wombats, 9
World of the Wolf, The, 121

Young, Stanley P., 117, 129